PITY PARTIERS

PITY PARTIERS

CELEBRATING YOUR FAILURES TO ACHIEVE YOUR BIGGEST WINS

DANIELA CARRASCO

NEW DEGREE PRESS

PITY PARTIERS

Celebrating Your Failures to Achieve Your Biggest Wins

ISBN   978-1-64137-923-6 *Paperback*
       978-1-64137-703-4 *Kindle Ebook*
       978-1-64137-705-8 *Ebook*

To myself.
May this book forever be proof anything
is possible if you truly want it.
Work hard. Stay determined. Be kind.
You are enough.

CONTENTS

---

*"Sweet are the uses of adversity,
which, like the toad, ugly and venomous,
wears yet a precious jewel in his head."*

—WILLIAM SHAKESPEARE

INTRODUCTION

———

In 2017 I packed up my whole life and went from glitzy, glittery Las Vegas to rainy, grungy Seattle. *Move to Seattle* they said. *It will be easy* they said. I was fooled.

I moved to the infamous Pacific Northwest with a confidence level of 110 percent. Seattle may be known for its gloomy weather, but it was all sunshine upon my arrival. I worked in a beautiful building in downtown Seattle for an amazing tech startup. I lived in a killer apartment with a wall-to-wall living room window with an unobstructed view of the water. Nothing could stop me! That is, until the storm came rolling in.

I joined the tech industry when everyone was talking about, breathing, and encouraging everyone to be part of this industry, as it was the next best thing. After three years at a small customer relationship management company in Las Vegas, I had learned the ropes of the software industry. I accomplished my goals and knew it was time to make moves. I lived at the heart of the hotel industry and desired something bigger.

I was determined to move to a tech hub. I wanted to be surrounded by people who wore company hoodies and be part of the infamous tech world. Seattle was the city I had my eye on, the home of Microsoft, Amazon, and endless Christmas trees. I began to research companies in the area and sent out my resume. After various interviews, I landed a job at a startup telecommunications company. I promise it was cooler than it sounds. When I say telecommunications, I do not mean the classic phone provider store at your local mall. This company was providing the opportunity to work in their headquarters alongside a world-class team of engineers, marketing experts, and colleagues who had gained experience working in admired companies. Going from a baby startup to a much more established company was a new and exciting challenge. I went all in.

Although telecommunication wasn't Amazon, the company was new, hip, and everything I was looking for. The two-floor office was located in downtown Seattle in a vintage high-rise building. It was the kind you see in movies with gold revolving doors and marble flooring. I was hired to help create a new customer success department. I was ready, excited, and making my big money moves. It was the company and position that would take my career to the next level. I felt like I had hit the jackpot. It was definitely a "Hey look ma, I made it" moment.

Life could not have been better. I had the job I always dreamed of and lived in an amazing apartment with hands-down the best view I have ever had. An unobstructed postcard-like view of the water at the top of the hill. My first week living in Seattle was amazing. My parents drove my car up from Las Vegas, as my best friend visited to welcome me to my new home. Shortly after moving, I turned twenty-seven years old. A couple of my best friends flew in to surprise me on my special day, and we had the best weekend celebration. Life was awesome. I was on cloud nine. That is, until one month later on March 14th.

It was a Tuesday, and I had woken up to my regular daily programming. I sipped my morning coffee in a comfy chair on the deck as I watched sailboats floating around the water. I listened to Beyoncé on my way to work and Nancy, the building concierge, called out her daily greeting.

"Good morning, honey! Have a grand day!"

It was a normal day. I checked emails in the morning, played ping pong for a mid-morning pick-me-up, and had lunch on our patio overlooking the city. I had just wrapped up an afternoon meeting when my boss suddenly asked to speak to me. He mentioned needing to meet upstairs, as all the meeting rooms downstairs were taken. As we walked up the stainless-steel staircase and approached the second floor, I noticed a couple of staff putting their desk items into small white cardboard boxes. I found it interesting but thought nothing of it. I thought perhaps they were moving desks.

As we walked to the conference rooms toward the back of the office, we made a sudden right turn into the HR offices. I was so confused as to why I was being led to HR. I instantly wondered *what did I do wrong?* I swear I signed all of my paperwork and only used my bus card for work purposes. As I walked into the office, the head of HR stood in front of the desk with tears in her eyes as she too held one small white cardboard box.

As we sat down in the meeting room, my boss began the conversation by apologizing for moving me out to Seattle. I was very confused because all I could think about was how happy I was. I had everything I had ever wanted. As he continued, his voice began to break. I personally thought he was coughing, but in reality, he was trying to hold back the tears. He continued on to say the company had faced financial challenges and half of the staff was going to be let go.

"Unfortunately, Daniela, I am going to need to let you go. The company no longer has the funds to create your department. I am so sorry, as I know you just moved your entire life to Seattle."

He continued talking, but all I heard was "I need to let you go," and "I am so sorry as I know you just moved your entire life to Seattle." I felt nothing, not even sadness. I went into shock and felt numb. I actually had a huge smile on my face and began to laugh. All that came out of my mouth was, "Okay. It's okay. I'll be okay. Thank you for the opportunity."

I was given the small cardboard white box and was asked to pack up my things and leave. I ditched the box, packed my three black pens and brown leather notebook into my backpack, and called an Uber to pick me up. Standing outside of what was once my dream office building, I lost it. Tears poured down my cheeks like water from an open faucet.

I got into the car and tried to hide my tears. I did not speak the entire drive home. The ride was only fifteen minutes long, but felt eternal as I struggled to hold back my tears. When I arrived home, I placed my backpack on the floor just as the tears began to roll in again. I sat down on the comfy chair on the deck. Strangely, the view did not look as beautiful as it had that morning. I sat there and cried for a solid two hours. My life got flipped upside down in a matter of hours.

Life sucked big time. I was jobless, friendless and, to top it off, moneyless. When you suddenly get let go from a job, there is no stimulus check to save you. You have to figure it out on your own. Although this could have been the start to a dark path, I took it as a new and exciting opportunity. Instead of curling up in a ball and giving up, I didn't quit. Mama didn't raise no quitter. I was in Seattle, home of the top tech companies and endless job opportunities. Although I had reached rock bottom, I was excited to see what this new city had in store.

Due to being brand new to the city, I had no network and zero friends. If there is one thing I gained from my sorority days, it was the art of recruiting. I put on my recruiting hat and joined every young professional group on Facebook, LinkedIn, and Meetup. Due to having an abundance of free time between completing job applications, I would attend every available event. As I began to meet people and make friends, the typical what-do-you-do-for-work question consistently came up. As I shared my story, one common question consistently kept surfacing:

"How are you so happy?"

Every time I would share my story of getting let go, they would be so surprised with my attitude. They viewed my optimistic attitude as an oxymoron to the situation.

"I don't know how you are doing it, because I'd be super sad or depressed if I were you."

Everyone teaches you to be successful, but very rarely are you taught how to cope when failure comes knocking on your door. At the end of the day I am human, and yes, the loss of what I thought was my dream job hurt me to the core. Rejection is never fun. Of course I had my moments of sadness and despair, but I only allowed those feelings to consume me during my three Pity Parties.

PITY PARTIES

Pity Parties are my personal method to overcome failure. When I was younger, my parents taught me life was going to be hard and was occasionally going to suck. I was never shielded from reality. To better understand my upbringing, you must know that I grew up in a very honest, unfiltered Mexican family. My parents tell it how it is. Being made aware of life's unpreventable curveballs, they taught me how to best react to it. My parents advised that when life introduced failures or setbacks, I was permitted three Pity Parties to react to the situation. During the three Pity Parties, I was allowed to do whatever I wanted; I could cry, eat, scream, whatever my heart desired and felt like I needed to do to truly feel the emotion. I was only allowed a total of three of these Pity Parties. After the third Pity Party, I had to wrap it up and move on. No excuses. I had to stand up and move on.

Everyone thinks happiness is defined by our successes and achievements, but I have realized that is not true. We are defined by how we react and respond to failure. It is not about you failing, but that you get back up. It's not about how you messed up, but acknowledging that you can be and do better. I have literally trained my brain to be happy and see the bright side of challenging situations. I have realized not everyone approaches tough situations the same way nor thinks the same as I do. What I have learned has made me realize I'm a Pity Partier... and as soon as we all embrace this, we can all learn to overcome and thrive after any failure.

Failure is guaranteed in life. Every single person on this Earth will fail in their lifetime. Let me say it again for the people in the back. Everyone from your manager, to your teachers, to your parents, to widely successful entrepreneurs have failed and will continue to do so. If you are not failing, you are not growing. If you are not growing, you are not stepping out of your comfort zone. The key to growth is to be aware of how failure affects us to manage it effectively.

The effect of failure begins at the very top: the brain. In an article published by Educational Advancement, upon experiencing a win, endorphins, dopamine, and serotonin are released, which encourage us to engage in a task again.[1] When we experience a failure, our brains release cortisol, also known as the stress hormone, which results in feeling a lack of acceptance and safety.[2] In connection with these feelings, one can also feel anxious, have negative thoughts, and get stressed.[3] High levels of cortisol result in an increase in your

---

1   Zadra Rose Ibañez, "WHAT HAPPENS WHEN YOU FAIL?" Institute For Educational Advancement, last modified April 10, 2018.

2   Ibid.

3   Sheri Jacobson, "Is this the Real Reason You Feel Like A Failure." *Harley Therapy Counselling Blog*, last modified September 26, 2017.

heart rate and blood pressure.[4] If those high levels persist, it can lead to chronic stress which can produce symptoms such as fatigue, headaches, anxiety, and depression.[5] According to the National Institute of Mental Health, major depressive disorder affects approximately 17.3 million American adults, or about 7.1 percent of the US population age eighteen and older, in a given year.[6]

Seattle is the city not only known for *Twilight* and the Space Needle, but also the gloomy weather and high depression rates. People living in Seattle between the ages of eighteen and thirty-four have a higher depression diagnosis rate at 5.1 percent compared to the national average of 4.4 percent.[7] No wonder people thought my positivity was so weird. I had arrived from Vegas, baby! Las Vegas, an oasis of indulgence that keeps the dice rolling until sunrise. The city of sun-filled, vibrant, colorful adult playgrounds.

Although it was a major day-to-night change, I have enjoyed every minute of it. If it weren't for my move, I would not be where I am today. Yes, it was a rocky start, but thanks to failure I have learned so much about myself, my strength, and my potential. I mean, I am writing a frickin' book! I have a true passion to help others on this topic. Failure should not be feared. Failure should be celebrated. I want to share my framework to help people and their relationship with failure.

---

4   "Beware High Levels of Cortisol, the Stress Hormone," Premier Health, last modified February 05, 2017.

5   Ibid.

6   "Major Depression," National Institute of Mental Health, last modified February 2019.

7   "Depression Diagnosis Rates are Increasing Across Washington, Study Finds," Premera Blue Cross, last modified May 10, 2018.

I truly believe that the moment you change your perspective towards failure is the day you unlock your greatest potential. Hence, I encourage you to become a Pity Partier.

I welcome everyone to the Pity Party. Therefore, this book is intended for anyone who has or is currently struggling to deal with failure. I'm going to be honest: I am all about women helping women. When I see women struggling with failure, especially those in their twenties and thirties, I just want to hold their hand and tell them to throw a Pity Party! This book is for them. No matter who you are or where you live, we share many of the same life experiences such as getting fired from a dream job, not reaching goals, break-ups, or being rejected. I have experienced failure with every single one of those situations, know how to approach them and bounce back. I believe in myself. Being resilient and getting back up after every fall led to me living a life I absolutely love and working a job I am actually excited for every day. I am confident, strong, and truly love myself. I wake up every day full of gratitude for every failure, because every single setback has molded me to be who I am today.

Now, I know I am not the only woman who has learned to embrace life's suckiness. I am surrounded by strong, inspiring, and successful queens who have used failure as driving fuel to build their path forward in their career, relationships, and life. Since too many books on the shelves highlight males, I wanted to focus my writing on highlighting stories from the ladies. I had the honor of interviewing a couple of women I highly admire. Throughout this book I will be sharing:

- How the founder of Sheila Bella Permanent Makeup and Microblading embraced her setbacks, which resulted in building a seven-figure company in three years.
- How a VP at iHeartMedia got to the executive leadership level at one of the top media companies in the US.
- On the topic of love, FNGR's Yoda Love Expert will share how her biggest failure in love led to unleash selflove.

The intention of this book is to provide the framework to redefine failure. I firmly believe failures are the foundation to bigger wins.

- If you are experiencing failure and feeling stuck, this is the book for you.
- If you need assistance to navigate failure, this is for you.
- If you have failed while trying to climb the corporate ladder, this is for you.
- If you have felt defeated, this is for you.
- If you are in need of someone to provide some honest truth, this is for you.

I too have felt lost. Trust me, I get it, and you are not alone. I do not come from a privileged family where everything was served up on a silver platter. It's actually the total opposite. I want to show how failures, and everything that comes along with it, can be overcome with Pity Parties.

- I will walk you through personal failures you hopefully resonate with.
- I will explain how I embraced defeat using this Pity Party Methodology.
- I will show you how you too can become a proud Pity Partier.
- I will share tips of how successful women have uncovered their own Pity Party Method.
- Lastly, I will provide Party Favors at the end of each chapter as takeaways.

Happiness is how we respond to failure. So be resilient, put on that party hat, and be a proud Pity Partier!

CHAPTER 1:

THE THREE PITY PARTIES

"Life is like a camera. Focus on what's important. Capture the good times. Develop from the negatives. And if things don't work out, take another shot."[8]

—UNKNOWN

Lesley Gore's song from 1963, "It's my party and I'll cry if I want to," has become my theme song.[9]

Everyone has a song that, upon listening, instantly takes them back to a vivid memory. These lyrics do that exact thing. I clearly remember listening to this iconic song the day before I took my

---

8   Paula Cameron, "13 UPLIFTING QUOTES FOR A SHINY HAPPY NEW YEAR," Wall Art Prints (website), last modified January 01, 2017.

9   *The Ed Sullivan Show*, "LESLEY GORE "It's My Party" on The Ed Sullivan Show," February 19, 2015, video, 1:12.

preschool pictures. The day I was introduced to the Pity Party Method is a fond memory not only for myself, but for my family. Every year this story gets brought up by my parents or brother at least once or twice. It is the reason behind why my family created the Pity Party Method to deal with failure.

Little Daniela had no idea this memory's lesson would persist throughout the years. However, my mama knew exactly what she was doing. "As your mama I wanted to teach you the value of not dwelling on situations or mistakes you make in life," she said, "My goal with this lesson was to teach you that when life knocks you down, you get back up. Feel whatever you need to feel, learn from the mistake, wrap it up, and keep on going."

THE HAIRCUT

It all began with a bowl haircut and bangs. I remember a handful of details, but the story has molded into a much clearer picture as my mama has shared her insight of that moment throughout the years. Picture day for my mama was like a pre–Super Bowl extravaganza. Mama bear would switch to coach mode every year as the day approached. I knew I was in for a fresh haircut, an on-point outfit, and polishing those creepy doll-like shoes she made me wear.

As per usual, she made an appointment at her friend Veronica's hair salon. Veronica was a sweet lady with a Brazilian blowout. Think Tyra Banks fashion show hair: straight, silky, and perfect. Unfortunately, my boy-like bowl haircut kept me far away from achieving that dream. I'm not sure why the nineties had such a fascination with the bowl style. Everyone had them at school, and all the moms thought they were adorable. I strongly disliked my hair, even more so because my older brother would tell me I looked like a boy.

Hoping to finally change my hairstyle, I was incredibly excited to get a haircut for the long-awaited preschool picture day.

As we arrived at the salon, I joyfully walked over to the black and silver chair and hopped onto the purple Barney bumper that added about six inches of height to the chair seat. Mama gave the haircut details to Veronica and I overheard her say, "I love it. She's going to look so cute!"

Veronica turned in my direction and asked if I was ready. *Ready,* I thought? *I was born ready!* She spun me away from the mirror and began to work her magic.

Once the haircut was done, the hair dryer was fired up and the round brush came out. As my hair was split into three, I noticed the reshaping of my bowl haircut. I felt betrayed. Again, I was facing picture day with the bowl on my head. What happened to us doing something different? I did gain a new set of bangs. Apparently, the bangs were the big "change."

Looking back now, the best way I can describe my haircut at the time is to compare it to Kuzco from *The Emperor's New Groove.* I did not like it. I dreaded having to show my face at school the next day with the hideous hairstyle. As we walked home, all I kept thinking was how I could get rid of those hideous bangs. My mama, of course, loved the new style. "Dani, your pink headband is going to look great," she exclaimed on the way home.

SNIP, SNIP!

I sat in my parent's bathroom and attempted to hide the bangs any way I could: pinning them back, adding gel, wax, hairspray, and used everything I could find in my mama's vanity. After many failed attempts, I sat on my parents' bed defeated because nothing worked. Out of nowhere, the grand idea popped into my head. If Veronica cut my hair to create bangs, I can cut my hair to get rid of them. Genius! What a smart cookie I was. I grabbed my mama's sewing scissors and attempted to recreate Veronica's cutting technique. I bundled the bangs with my right hand, twisted them, and cut as close as I could to my forehead to completely get rid of them. As I snipped away, I saw the bangs disappear. It was like magic. One minute they were there, and the other they were gone. I peeked into the mirror and marveled at how much better I looked without the bangs.

My four-year-old self thought it was perfect and beautiful. I was so proud of myself, but I also knew what I had done was not right. Of course, I did everything to avoid getting in trouble. My next move was to hide the evidence, which I definitely learned from watching *Cops* with my older brother. I could not allow my mama to discover my chopped hair in the trash can. I knew I had to hide the hair. I scanned the room for a good hiding spot. Bingo: behind the heavy cabinet pushed against the wall. Genius! My mama could not possibly find it there. I gathered the hair, bundled it, and tossed it over the edge between the cabinet and the wall.

As I was cleaning up the area, Mama called me to the kitchen. I strolled into the kitchen with a little pep in my step, beaming with confidence. I knew I looked good and Mama was going to approve. I stood in the kitchen doorway while Mama stood in front of the stove moving a pot away from the burner. She was mid-sentence when she suddenly looked up and saw me. She instantly screamed, "Daniela, what did you do to your hair?"

My mama's use of my full name instead of "Dani" was a major red flag. I knew I was in big trouble. I stood there in shock, confused at how she had failed to see the masterpiece I had created out of my hair. She quickly turned off the stove and knelt down to assess the damage.

"What have you done? Why did you do this? Picture day is tomorrow," she said in an angry tone.

Angry mama rarely made an appearance, but when she did, it was scary. The lady is five-foot-nothing, but she is your typical feisty, sassy, Mexican mom. I instantly knew my "genius" plan had failed. She sent me to my room and told me to wait for her. I knew what awaited me. It was the one thing every child dreaded: a spanking. After the spanking, I sat in my room crying for what felt like hours. After some time passed, Mama asked me to come to the living room.

My mama came in, sat down next to me, and explained the reason she was so furious was because I had ruined the freshly styled hair she had spent hard-earned money on. I do have to explain that money at that time was tight. My parents were very cautious when it came to expenses. Due to this, Mama was not pleased when she saw my Edward Scissorhands-like job. She said what I had done was wrong, as it was going to cost her an additional money to fix. This may not seem like a big deal to some people, but letting my mama down was like giving my heart a paper cut. Mama's disappointment stung deeply. I was a good kid who followed the rules. I always strove to make my parents proud.

THE THREE PITY PARTIES

As I woke up the next day, I remembered what I had done. The tears came rolling down. When Mama heard me crying, she rushed into my room and asked what was wrong. I explained I was sad because of what I had done to my bangs. My mama is the most caring lady on earth, but she knows how to drop some truth when you need it most. She didn't know it, but the words that came out of her mouth would follow me through all of the struggles and failures I would face in my life.

"Dani, you need to stop crying. You cannot cry forever. You are allowed three Pity Parties. You can do anything you want during these Pity Parties; you can cry, stomp your feet, or whine. However, after the third one you need to wipe those tears, wash your face, and move on. No more tears after that third Pity Party."

Pity Party I thought. That was a new set of words for my four-year-old brain. I asked her the meaning of the two words. From what I understood, pity was taking action to feel your feelings and party was taking action to celebrate your feelings and move on with your life. As I grew older, my mama reinforced this idea of throwing a Pity Party and I learned to associate it with success.

I followed Mama's direction and threw my Pity Parties. All the parties were to be taken place while alone. I assume this was part of my punishment, as I was not allowed to play with my big brother. As Mama instructed, my Pity Parties were to be broken into three parts:

Pity Party One: Feeling sad. My mama always encouraged me to truly feel my emotions because she did not want me to avoid them. If you numb sadness, you numb joy. As she says, "Let it all out. Release everything you have in order to make room for finer things." I went to bed and wallowed in the sadness of what I had done.

Pity Party Two: Disappointment. As a kid who was a people pleaser and followed every rule, disappointing my mama was upsetting. I felt ashamed she had to spend extra money to fix my hair.

Pity Party Three: Anger. Despite what I had done, I still thought it was unfair that I had been punished for my masterful haircut. I stomped around my room to release the steam.

I began to cry again. As Mama listened, she reminded me it was my third one.

"Dani, last one. I do not want to hear it after this," she said.

With tears covering my cheeks, I realized what I had done was not correct. I learned my lesson: I cannot cut my hair without Mama's permission. I followed her instructions. I went to the bathroom, washed my face, and wiped it dry as I overcame the last Pity Party. My mama came into the bathroom, gave me a big hug, and declared it was time to move on. I remember her praising me for completing the Pity Parties. "You did it! And look, you're fine. We had a little bump on the road, but you are good now," she told me.

The next step after the third Pity Party was to take action towards a solution. I made a mistake; I allowed myself to acknowledge the feelings, released them, and now it was time to move on. We focused on finding a solution for my not-so-great idea of chopping my hair. I had small hairs sticking out of my forehead like a porcupine. It was comical. I remember us standing in front of Mama's vanity with an array of hair products covering the tabletop. Mama applied gel, hairspray, pomade, and every product she could get her hands on. She attempted a ponytail, a low ponytail, a half ponytail, and a headband. The styles were endless. We finally went for the one that made me look somewhat acceptable. We both laughed as we realized how ridiculous I looked. We eventually went with a weird top bun on the side of my head that made me look like a pineapple. I remember us laughing so much as we tried to figure out what side looked best for the upcoming photo shoot. Now, I look back at that preschool picture and giggle about the whole situation.

"See Dani, you went from tears to laughter. You made a mistake, but you're okay now," Mama said.

I thought *ah, from tears to laughter. That is a Pity Party!* I associated failures with Pity Parties and celebrations. My mama's affirmation that I was okay stuck with me. This event's impact even surprises my mama sometimes. As I've grown to adulthood, she has often mentioned, "I never imagined the haircut incident would teach you so much. Seeing you incorporate the Pity Parties as you got older made me realize the power of this method."

No matter how big I failed, I was going to be okay. Little did my mama know the Three Pity Party Method would be a lesson I would carry forever. The older I got, the more failures I experienced—failing my first exam, failing my first class, failing to get a role in the school play, and my first heartbreak. I am thirty years old, and to this day I use this Three Pity Party Method when the road to success is paved with failure or life throws curveballs. Of course, my failures now are larger than a simple haircut incident.

I have failed at:

- Meeting revenue and quota goals at work by being a handful of dollars short.
- Getting a promotion after working late hours and weekends trying to prove I was deserving.
- Relationships by not respecting my personal standards.
- Passing a test or class at school.

Adult failures can be much more life altering in comparison to childhood failures, but the fact I celebrate each of them does not change. The end goal is the same, which is to stand back up and move on. To this day I allow myself three Pity Parties. After the third one, I wash my face and get going. I hope the stories and Party Favors I share within this book will provide a template to also use the Three Pity Party Method as a roadmap to success. Welcome to the party!

CHAPTER 2:

THE SCIENCE
OF FAILURE

———

"It's failure that gives you the proper perspective on success."[10]
—*ELLEN DEGENERES*

Success is invited, but failure is not. Success tends to be attributed to celebration while failure is accredited to breakdowns. We are constantly reminded of success with awards, grades, and glorified social media posts. Rarely are we shown the transparency of failures. I see this all the time with my friends, and I am also guilty of it. Our social media accounts consist of pretty pictures illustrating amazing travels, engagements, new car purchases, and baby announcements. Posts about divorces, miscarriages, or unemployment are infrequent. I personally did not create a post when I got let go from a job or the time my relationship ended upon

———

10 Ekaterina Walter, "30 Powerful Quotes on Failure," *Forbes*, last modified December 30, 2013.

realizing my significant other and I had grown apart. My reasoning was no one wants to see that. I did not want to have people feel bad for me or ruin their day with my sappy story. These events did not align with the "cultural happiness" most commonly showcased. We tend to conceal our failures from the world.

Failure is associated with negative emotions which go hand-in-hand with feelings and ideas of defeat, frustration, and disappointment. We have all heard the expression "I feel like a failure." Feeling like a failure is like a stab to the gut. It is painful. I wish I could say you are special and will forever be protected from failing, but that would be a lie. While failure does hurt, it is essential. If you are not failing, you are not growing. As motivational speaker Rachel Hollis states, "We become who we're meant to be when we fall and rise again."[11]

Due to the inevitability of failure, I was interested in digging deeper on the subject. What happens internally when we experience failure? Understanding the science behind failure and the effects it has on our brain, emotions, and why we typically struggle with it is important. Failure can be a great catalyst for change. Instead of allowing failure to deter us, we can better understand how to approach it.

---

11   *Rachel Hollis.* "The BEST Way To Start The New Year in 2020." December 26, 2019, video, 3:46.

LET'S TALK ABOUT THE BRAIN, BABY!

Starting from the top, it should be to no surprise that it all begins with the brain. Upon experiencing a win, like a promotion, our brain releases "happy chemicals" such as endorphins, dopamine, and serotonin, which encourage us to perform a task again.[12] When we experience a failure, like not reaching a goal, our brains release cortisol, commonly known as the "stress hormone," which does not leave us with the emotional response of acceptance and safety.[13] Cortisol increases the relative right frontal activity which can be seen as the "control panel" of our personality and our ability to communicate.[14] Results of an EEG study that investigated the effects of cortisol administration in eight healthy volunteers found a reduction in approach motivation, and was associated with anxiety, distress, and nervousness.[15] High cortisol levels can hurt you more than they can help you. If the stress response fails to shut off and reset, it can lead to depression.[16]

Unfortunately, we are all human and cannot escape stress. Stress can be experienced at work, at home, in relationships, and even on the road. Stress can be identified in two groups: acute stress which is "short term" or chronic stress

---

12   Zadra Rose Ibañez, "What Happens When you Fail," Institute For Educational Advancement, last modified April 10, 2018.

13   Ibid.

14   "Front Lobe," Healthline, accessed May 31, 2020.

15   Watchara Sroykham, and Yodchanan Wongsawat, "Effects of Brain Activity, Morning Salivary Cortisol, and Emotion Regulation on Cognitive Impairment in Elderly People," *Medicine* vol. 98,26 (2019): e16114.

16   Karen Bruno, "Stress and Depression," WebMd, accessed November 12, 2019.

which is "long term."[17] Acute stress can be experienced by situations involving unpredictability or a threat to the ego.[18] They can be mild stressors like when your alarm clock goes off in the morning, being pulled over for speeding, or even a phone call that needs to be answered when you are relaxing and watching Netflix. Chronic stress is the response to emotional pressure and is experienced for a prolonged period.[19] Chronic stress prompts feelings of having little or no control.[20] If you are struggling with finances, a severe illness, or consistently working overtime, the stress can become chronic. These types of long-term aggravations can leave you stressed for months or even more than a year. Chronic stress puts wear-and-tear on your body and mind, leading to an increased risk of experiencing depression.[21]

If you have trouble coping with a negative situation, it can lead to overwhelming chronic stress. The constant worry and negative thoughts can lead to loss of interest and become a factor in the introduction of depression.[22] According to the American Psychiatric Association, "depression is a common and serious medical illness that negatively affects how

---

17 Elizabeth Scott, "All About Acute Stress What You Should Know About Acute Stress," VeryWellMind, last modified April 08, 2020.

18 Ibid.

19 Elizabeth Scott, "How Does Chronic Stress Negatively Affect Your Health?" VeryWellMind, last modified October 10, 2019.

20 Ibid.

21 Ibid.

22 Ibid.

you feel, the way you think, and how you act."[23] Feeling sad, loss of energy, guilt, and loss of interest in activities once enjoyed are common symptoms of depression.[24] It can affect people emotionally, physically and in everyday tasks such as functioning at work and home.[25] According to the National Institute of Mental Health, major depressive disorder affects approximately 17.3 million American adults, or about 7.1 percent of the US population age eighteen and older, in a given year.[26]

FEAR OF FAILING

Self-isolation due to fear of failure could possibly result in depression. Untreated depression and anxiety can lead to a sense of powerlessness that arises from repeatedly stressful situations, also known as learned helplessness.[27] In the worst case scenario, atychiphobia, the overwhelming and extreme fear of failure, may be experienced.[28] Atychiphobia affects between 2 and 5 percent of the American population.[29] Being aware of this, it is important to keep an eye on common symptoms that lead to fearing failure.

---

23 "What Is Depression," Depression, American Psychiatric Association, accessed November 12, 2019.

24 Ibid.

25 Ibid.

26 "Major Depression," National Institute of Mental Health, last modified February 2019.

27 Tamara Hill, "Atychiphobia: 3 Signs You Fear Failure," Caregivers, Family & Friends, PsychCentral, last modified December 04, 2018.

28 Ibid.

29

Common symptoms of the fear of failure include:[30]

- Hesitation to try new things.
- Self-sabotage—For example, procrastination, extreme anxiety, or a failure to complete goals.
- Low self-esteem or self-confidence—Commonly using negative statements.
- Perfectionism—Only pursuing things you know you will finish perfectly and successfully.

SHAME

No one wants to be seen as a failure but experiencing failure itself is not always a bad thing. Failure is the source of growth. Let's take a look at Vera Wang, one the most talented and prominent bridal designers. Did you know Vera Wang's original dream was not rooted in fashion? She was actually on the road to become a professional figure skater but failed to make the US Olympics team in 1986.[31] Due to that event, she went into retail by working at a Yves Saint Laurent boutique in New York. Upon entering the fashion world, she uncovered a new talent. She moved on to work at *Vogue,* Ralph Lauren, and eventually created her fashion empire. Upon being ask about failure, Wang said, "When you fall down—which you have to do if you want to learn to be a skater—you pick yourself right up and start again. You don't let anything deter you."[32] This reason is why we should not be afraid of failure. So why do people cringe when the act or feeling of failure is mentioned? Psychologist and author Guy

---

30 "Overcoming Fear of Failure Facing Your Fear of Moving Forward," Mind Tools, Emerald Works, accessed November 12, 2019.

31 Rosa Christopher and Samantha Leach , "12 Famous Women on Facing—and Overcoming—Failure," *Glamour,* last modified January 29, 2019.

32 Ibid.

Winch explains the reason why people are afraid of failure is that they are actually afraid of feeling deep shame: "Shame is a psychologically toxic emotion because instead of feeling bad about our actions (guilt) or our efforts (regret), shame makes us feel bad about who we are. Shame gets to the core of our egos, our identities, our self-esteem, and our feelings of emotional well-being."[33]

The concept of encapsulating failure as shame was first introduced to most of us when we entered elementary school. We were taught good grades got us ahead and bad grades kept us behind. A's got you center on the fridge while F's got you a seat in detention. If you received a good grade you would be prized with a sticker, button, or additional recess time. However, if you received F's you were shamed as the "bad kid" in class who had fun activities taken away as punishment. Everyone would show off being on the honor roll, but no one would show off being the child who failed.

When we shake off the shame, we learned to associate it with failure. It can therefore work in our favor. Take the hilarious comedian Tina Fey. Every time I see one of her *Saturday Night Live* skits, I get tears of laughter. However, the audience was not always laughing when she began her career in comedy. Tina states, "For my first show at *SNL*, I wrote a Bill Clinton sketch, and during our read-through, it wasn't getting any laughs. This weight of embarrassment came over me, and I felt like I was sweating from my spine out. But I realized, "Okay that happened, and I did not die."

---

33   Guy Winch, "10 Signs That You Might Have Fear of Failure," *Psychology Today*, last modified June 18, 2013.

You've got to experience failure to understand that you can survive it."[34] As Tina Fey says it, you can and will survive failure. For example, I personally celebrate my failures with a Pity Party. Pity Parties tend to be seen as unacceptable, but I actually view them as stepping stones to build resilience against negative events and emotions.

RESILIENCE

Resilience, the ability to recover from or adjust easily to misfortune or change, is not a magical power people are born with.[35] It is a trait involving behaviors, thoughts, and actions that can be learned and developed. When a person is resilient, it does not mean they do not experience difficulties. It actually means they experience failures but see them as helpful feedback to grow from and develop a different perspective.

Some of the first researchers to investigate resilience were child psychologists Emmy E. Werner and Ruth Smith.[36] Werner and Smith conducted a forty-year-long study on the development of 698 infants born in 1955 on the Hawaiian island of Kauai. The study tracked and recorded how each participant handled setbacks and adversity in their lives, and their ultimate success. In general, Werner and Smith found that their sample of children faced adverse conditions as they grew, such as mental illness, poverty, parents who had

---

34 Rosa Christopher and Samantha Leach, "12 Famous Women on Facing—and Overcoming—Failure," *Glamour,* last modified January 29, 2019.

35 Merriam-Webster.com Dictionary, s.v. "resilience (n.)," accessed April 16, 2020.

36 "About Resilience," Devereux Center For Resilient Children, accessed May 27, 2020.

not graduated from high school, and unstable family environments.[37] The majority of the children developed serious problems of their own by age ten. However, to the researchers' revelation, about one-third of the children living under these conditions led successful lives. Those who experienced difficulties such as delinquencies and mental health problems during their teenage years had become successful, functioning adults. The research identified the key factors that made someone more well-adjusted, resilient, and successful than those who struggled.

The building blocks to resiliency researchers recommended, which you can add to your tool chest to become more well-adjusted, included:[38]

- Continue to seek autonomy—You are able to make your own choices and go your own direction.
- Seek out new experiences—Get out of your comfort zone and try something new.
- Actively lean on the right people—Seek out a mentor or people whom you admire. Build your tribe.
- Lead a self-determined life—You have control over your own life.
- Apply a healthy mix of pragmatism and possibility—Rely on your self-confidence.
- Be good at being good-natured—Be kind.

---

37 Bobbi Emel, "Learning from Resilient Kids," Psych Central, last modified October 08, 2018.
38 Scott Mauz, "This Remarkable 32-Year Study of Kauai Islanders Reveals 7 Keys to Living a Resilient Life," *Inc.*, last modified June 13, 2018.

Developing resilience looks very different for everyone as people react differently to stressful situations. I wish I can say it is as easy as waving a magic wand, but I am not your fairy godmother, nor we do not live inside a Disney movie. The approach to building resilience may work for one person, but not for others. Begin with one building block. Take it one step at a time and just try. To be honest, it took a while to figure out what worked for me. During my bigger failures, it was hard to be resilient because I was so hurt. However, with the help of my supportive friends, I kept going and picking myself back up. The people with whom you surround yourself are a big key factor here. I am extremely particular on who I surround myself with. I am not kidding. I am like a Las Vegas club bouncer who does not let just anyone in. The reason is because I am adamant about protecting my peace. If the person is not going to help me to become a better version of myself, they are out. You take in energy from the people with whom you surround yourself. If someone is not helping you to become the best version of yourself, tell them goodbye.

Throughout this book, I will walk you through my personal tricks of building resiliency and you will understand why I preach about this. When failure is faced, I throw myself a party. Yes, I actually celebrate the fact that I failed. Throughout many experiences in my life, I have learned to be failure's friend, because it has actually made me stronger. We cannot avoid failure; we have to embrace it. So, let your hair down, grab those tissues, get comfy, and throw yourself a Pity Party.

CHAPTER 3:

BURN THE BOAT

—

"The road to success is paved with failure. Every time you're knocked out of your routine, you're put into a state of discomfort. That's when your greatest milestones occur. That's when the greatest growth happens. That's where wisdom is born."

—SHEILA BELLA

The value of failure is expressed perfectly by the woman whose failures led her to build a seven-figure business within three years.

As I began to brainstorm ideas for this book, I wanted to focus on sharing my Pity Party Method and provide a framework to overcoming failure. The more I thought about this topic, I realized I could not be the only person who has their own personal method. Other people have their own similar method for Pity Parties, and I wanted the 4-1-1.

Comparing your first chapter with someone else's tenth chapter is very easy. We have all been there. You see someone thriving at a certain thing and decide to give it a try.

You go all in, give it a shot, and immediately compare your results with theirs. Quickly, you realize you are not at their level and begin to think it is impossible to reach their success. Perhaps you think they have a superpower you are lacking. Nope, that is not it. The reason the results are not the same is because you are at the beginner level and the other person is at the intermediate or expert level. It takes extreme effort to achieve something outrageously extraordinary.

This got me thinking of successful women I admire who started from the bottom and advanced to become CEOs, business owners, and leaders within their communities and in corporate settings. They all did not automatically obtain those titles because they rubbed a magic lamp. Studying the setback of others can help us navigate to avoid the same mistakes. I knew my first candidate had to be the one and only Sheila Bella. I was lucky to sit down with this brilliant, beautiful soul to talk about life and the many failures she has experienced.

In case you are not a makeup fanatic like myself, here's some quick insight about Sheila, a famous, successful ball of energy. Sheila is the type of person you meet and instantly want to become best friends with. I am not exaggerating. Ten minutes into our Zoom call, she practically got added to my bestie list. She is that one friend who just tells it how it is. She is full of positivity, and her Instagram pep talks make you feel like a million bucks by the end. Sheila is very transparent and proudly displays her failures to her online tribe. She may be making seven figures now, but her first chapter did not begin that way.

HARD WORK

Sheila was born in Quezon City, Philippines, and moved with her family to the United States at the young age of eight. In the chase for the American dream, they left everything they had to obtain everlasting opportunities for prosperity and success. Living in a two-bedroom apartment in Los Angeles with ten other people, Sheila saw her father take the family from an impoverished life to becoming homeowners in a middle-class neighborhood. Her father went from selling refurbished tools out of his van to owning his own tool shop. Sheila credits her immigrant father with the business skills she gained as he built several successful businesses from his hard work and dedication. Upon describing her family, she mentioned, "Hard work and chasing dreams are in my blood."

This lady has not been shy with trying new things. Her career includes everything from waitressing, to acting, to modeling. She was even crowned Miss Philippines USA in 2004 and has performed in numerous musical theater shows.[39] To say the least, she has done everything under the sun. Shelia's path to success was littered with difficulties before she became one of the first innovators in microblading in the United States and one of Los Angeles' first permanent makeup artists. She is now founder Sheila Bella Microblading, a widely famous business in the permanent makeup sector which caters to over fifteen thousand clients.

---

39 "SHEILA BELLA Founder & Lead Artist," Sheila Bella, accessed April 17, 2020.

FROM AVOCADO FRIES TO EYEBROWS

Building a seven-figure business was not done overnight. It has taken her over fifteen years to become the successful business owner she is today. Yes, you read that correctly— it took her fifteen years. Due to Sheila being positive and as bubbly as a glass of champagne, many people assume failure is an unknown subject to her. This is actually quite the opposite. Sheila has faced endless failures and fears throughout her life such as breaking through an unknown industry, starting a business, getting fired, managing a team, and experiencing imposter syndrome. As her story unfolds below, you will discover how Sheila has embraced tough situations life has thrown her way with her secret ingredient, which is to not personify failure. She described it as such:

"If you are feeling uncomfortable right now, if all of a sudden life is harder for you right now, congratulations! It means you are leveling up and on the road to success."

In my conversation with Sheila, we got to the good stuff: the curveballs and detours she experienced during her early stages. The day Sheila stumbled upon the idea of permanent makeup; she was actually waiting tables at Dillon's Irish Pub in Hollywood. Because the job required her to wear a full face of makeup every day, she gave microblading a try and fell in love. Although the job allowed her to pay the bills, she desired to do more than serve avocado fries in a schoolgirl outfit. That desire became more of a reality upon getting fired from the waitressing job. She was not passionate about it and, according to Sheila, she was not good at it. She describes this time by saying, "God put me in a place with no safety net, and I had to burn the boat. If there is no net, you will fly. I trusted that I was going to turn into the woman I needed to be." Necessity makes you act. She burned the boat to truly find the courage to push herself to bigger and better things.

Upon determining her next move, Sheila recalled her permanent makeup experience. She greatly enjoyed it and realized she could also become an artist. She decided to step into the permanent makeup industry. Since she was jobless, she had nothing to lose. Sheila went all in. She knew she could take the service to the next level. When the industry kicked off, only older women like our grandmas would get their eyebrows tattooed. As my friends in Oklahoma would say, "Bless their hearts." Old-school permanent makeup consisted of harsh lines and permanent marker-like art drawn on the face. It was not natural-looking nor easy on the eye. Sheila recalls her friends not being supportive of the new path she chose when she mentions, "People told me that my plan to tattoo faces for a living sounded like a shallow and vapid career that would never catch on."

She was determined to repackage and re-market the service to attract girls her age. She signed up for a five-day permanent makeup course, and the journey began.

FACING FAILURE

Sheila recalls shutting down the opinions of those surrounding her because she was determined to make it work.

She graduated from the makeup course and decided to kick off her business. However, there was a big problem—she did not have any customers. Sheila put on her heels and went in search for customers. She explains this was the moment the rejections began. She knocked on doors of businesses with the hope of a partnership and was turned away countless times. She went to local malls and hair salons to request her brochure be displayed at checkout counters, and again she was rejected. However, every rejection taught Sheila a very valuable lesson. She learned to detach her feelings from failure and see it as a learning opportunity. As Sheila explained, she does not allow herself to personify her failures.

"I think people are afraid of failure because it embodies them. They attach their personal worth to the failure too much instead of looking at it as just something to learn from. It's just a mistake. It's not that big of a deal."

Sheila had to constantly swallow her pride, but kept going. For every nine people that would turn her down, one would agree to work with her. It turned her into what she describes as a shameless self-promoter, but she learned to own this definition because she "felt shame all the time, but if I meditated on those feelings I wasn't going to get anywhere."

Although Sheila did not have an instant group of fans, she kept going. Failure was not an option. She learned from every "no" and paved her road to success, one failure after the other. She became stronger along the way. She saw every setback as a new opportunity. Although failing was not fun, she described not allowing it to define her:

"I knew I was not the smartest person. However, I was the most hardworking. I learned to make things work."

FILLING THE APPOINTMENT BOOK

Sheila's first year in business was the most challenging, yet the most rewarding. She did not have the funds to hire a web designer or staff to take her calls. She worked with what she had and made it happen. She mentioned learning HTML by spending ten to sixteen hours on YouTube to create her own website. She pretended to be her own receptionist when clients called to make it seem as if it was an established business. Sheila recalls recording her business's voicemail greeting under the bed covers with spa music in the background to make it sound more professional. She built everything she needed with the available resources. She did not allow any excuse to slow her down.

Sheila began to plaster her business on social media and joined local chambers of commerce to network. Only a few clients were gained, but the small traction did not stop her from working even harder. She continued to market herself. As time went by, she received more phone calls and the appointment book began to get filled. She wasn't making millions by any means, but she was making enough money to get by. She thought back to her original idea of repackaging permanent makeup services to attract a younger demographic.

Sheila decided to make video content of the procedure to demonstrate how her art was done. She reached out to her waitress friends at Dillon's and offered a free service in exchange for them being highlighted in a video. Sheila set the stage for the targeted demographic as she built her portfolio. The more she shared on social media, the more people began to pay attention. Suddenly, influencers on social media began to reach out and request her services. Sheila's business quickly gained traction.

The traction continued as she kept working hard, failing, and getting back up. She slowly became an industry leader in presenting permanent makeup as something more natural and beautiful. Sheila was able to change young people's perceptions of permanent makeup. Fast-forward fifteen years, Sheila still continues to embrace her failures and grows from every single one of them. When I asked her about her secret to preventing failure from dragging someone down, she said, "I think the secret to failure is you just can't take it too personally, and to just know that it's the only way to reach success."

Success is what Sheila has continued to achieve. Leading a prosperous seven-figure beauty business, host of The MakeUp Podcast, the number one permanent podcast on iTunes, a global success speaker, business coach, and now the creator of the first-ever Pretty Ambitious Summit, Sheila's new goal is to extend her hand and help other women reach the success she has achieved. As we wrapped up our conversation, I asked Sheila what advice she would give to those currently struggling to overcome failure, and she responded:

"Burn the boat, do not personify your failure, and stop playing small."

Party Favors:

- DO NOT LET FAILURES DEFINE YOU. JUST BECAUSE YOU FAILED DOES NOT MAKE YOU ANY LESS VALUABLE THAN THE PERSON NEXT TO YOU. LEARN FROM THE EXPERIENCE AND STAND BACK UP. EVERY SETBACK IS A GOLDEN NUGGET THAT LEADS YOU TOWARD A NEW DIRECTION.
- GET COMFORTABLE BEING UNCOMFORTABLE. CHANGE IS GOING TO BE TOUGH, BUT THE FASTER YOU GET COMFORTABLE WITH THE PROCESS, THE FASTER YOU WILL CHANGE YOUR PERSPECTIVE.
- KEEP GOING AND DO NOT GIVE UP. AS YOU READ, IT TOOK SHEILA FIFTEEN YEARS TO GET TO HER SEVEN-FIGURE DREAM. IF SHE WOULD HAVE GIVEN UP THE SECOND OR EVEN FIFTH YEAR IN, SHE WOULD HAVE MISSED OUT ON ALL OF THE GRAND OPPORTUNITIES SHE IS CURRENTLY LIVING WITH. KEEP GOING NO MATTER HOW HARD IT GETS. AS THEY SAY, ROME WAS NOT BUILT IN A DAY.

CHAPTER 4:

PITY PARTIER PRINCIPLE: RESILIENCE

——

"Life is not easy. Life is not fair. Life owes you nothing. Suck it up and move on. Nothing lasts forever."

—ABUELITO

No matter how hard life gets, you have to continue to stand up and move forward. Perseverance is key. This is a valuable lesson my abuelito, also known as grandpa, taught me at a young age. Resiliency, a principle of a true Pity Partier.

I come from a united, loving, imperfect, yet very honest, Mexican family. They are strong, hardworking, kind, and will not cut you any slack. In saying that, our family has no filter whatsoever, and the truth is spoken no matter if feelings get hurt. Tough skin is built into my DNA.

The pillar and leader of my family was my abuelito. Like many people, I have such fond memories of him. Although everyone says their grandpa was the best, mine truly was. What made him so extraordinary was his authentic personality, the raw love he expressed to everyone in his life, and the valuable teachings he engraved in us. His stories are my inheritance, and a reminder to be comfortable with the uncomfortable. My abuelito taught us to be resilient warriors, to recover quickly, and keep going.

The reason why he was such an advocate of resiliency was because he did not have an easy life. He experienced tragic moments which altered his perspective when it came to failure. Every time I visited, he would retell the story of his mom that forever changed his life. When Abuelito was four years old, his mother suddenly passed away. Her cause of death is forever unknown. What he did know was he would never see his mom again.

Have you ever witnessed a little boy lose his mom in a public area? The moment he realizes mom is out of sight, he begins to walk around the area. He looks up in search of his mom, but all he sees is a herd of strangers. The search continues, and the look of fear in his eyes becomes more apparent. His eyes get bigger and rounder as panic consumes him. He yells, "Mom, Mom, Mom!" and receives only silence as a response. His voice gets louder and shaky. He continues to search. Panic leads to tears and an overwhelming sadness over his mom potentially being gone forever. That sadness is temporary until he finds his mom. Once found, he instantly changes his demeanor, and peace washes away the feeling of panic.

Now imagine that panic being everlasting and having hours go by as the panic increases day by day. That exact feeling is what my abuelito experienced. He felt lost, lonely, and angry at life. He did not understand why God had placed such a tragedy in his path at such a young age.

A few days after his mom's death, he went back to school. Upon arriving, his teacher ridiculed him in front of all of his classmates because his uniform cardigan was missing a button. He recalled her saying, "Jorge, why is your sweater missing a button? Do you not have a mom that can sew?"

He began to cry as the teacher mocked him. He was facing his reality. No, he no longer had a mom. As my abuelito stood there in tears, his best friend stood up to defend him, "Miss, his mom passed away a couple of days ago."

The teacher quickly realized how hurtful her words had been toward my abuelito. She grabbed a few cents from her purse, apologized, and told him to go buy a piece of candy from the school store. As Abuelito walked out of that classroom with drooped shoulders and his head down, he realized his mom was gone forever. No more hugs. No more kisses. He told me he cried for days, weeks, until he realized his tears were not going to bring his mom back.

COPE AND RECOVER

From Abuelito's memory, he recalls his aunts consoling him, but that was temporary as everyone eventually went back to their normal lives after the funeral. As he got older, the grieving continued. Due to his father being distant at the time, he felt very alone and abandoned. He realized he had two choices: cheer himself up or keep on waiting indefinitely for someone else to make his life happier. He became his own cheerleader. Every time he felt sad, he would cheer himself up by listing things that made him happy. Every time he realized life was hard without his mom, he would see how far he had come all on his own. Giving up and staying down was not an option, as he had his whole life ahead of him. Abuelito taught himself to be really good at standing back up. Cope in spite of the setbacks.

Abuelito used that tragic event to learn an important lesson that is now our family motto: nothing lasts forever. Failure is not eternal unless you allow it to be. Learn from the pain, get up, and keep on moving forward. Every time I visited him, he'd say,

"When you fall, you have two choices: stay down or get back up. Stand up no matter how hard it is."

Upon experiencing failure, do something about it. Please do not give up just because it gets hard. Wake up people—life is supposed to be hard. Just think of the people who would have never made history had they allowed their failures to stop them. Take Abraham Lincoln, for example. We know him as our sixteenth president and a great figure in American history. Prior to reaching his success, he experienced an abundance of setbacks such as being defeated for political office multiple times, the death of his mother at a young age, and a failed business, just to name a few.[40] No matter how many times Lincoln failed, he was persistent and said, "My great concern is not whether you have failed, but whether you are content with your failure."[41]

LIFE IS FULL OF CHALLENGES

Abuelito had to be resilient throughout his life. As he went into adulthood, he kept this mentality of moving forward no matter how difficult life got. Just like every one of us, he faced multiple failures, setbacks, and tough situations. One failure he was very transparent about was his problem with alcohol. Abuelito was an alcoholic at one point in his life. He was not proud of it, but he most definitely did not deny it because the experience taught him so much.

From a young age, it was always Abuelito's dream to own a successful welding company. With the help of his resiliency, that dream became a reality. He founded his company, established two business locations, and only worked with elite companies in Mexico. He traveled the country leading projects and made a very good living. You can say he was a wealthy man who had it all—money, cars, a big family, and a nice home. With the abundance of success came an abundance of stress, peer pressure, and being surrounded by the wrong crowd.

Since alcohol was the main guest at every business meeting, he began to drink more often. More often became one to two drinks, then turned into an all-day affair. Slowly but surely

---

40   Harry Kierbow, "7 Famous Quotes on Failure and the Stories That Inspired Them," GoSmallBiz, last modified April 15, 2015.

41   Ibid.

alcohol took over his life physically, mentally, and emotionally. He had become dependent on it and quickly lost clients, projects, and one of his business locations.

He was failing both in every aspect of his business and with his family. Abuelito went from being the perfect father to the absent father. He stopped being present at home due to consistently blacking out at the office. Instead of taking part in family dinners, he spent the evenings at bars. The house, once filled with laughter, became full of arguments and tears. Abuelito explained how he would wake not knowing what day it was. He mentioned being aware of his situation, but he would cope by using alcohol to numb the embarrassment of facing his reality. That is until one day while being hungover at the office, his best friend gave him a dose of hard truth by saying, "What are you doing with your life? You are about to lose everything. Your family needs you. Do you realize that your actions are leading your kids to feel the same abandonment you felt when you lost your mom?"

As he heard that message, Abuelito realized how much pain he was not only putting on his wife, but most importantly his kids. He remembered feeling lost and unloved the day his mom died. He imagined his own children feeling the exact same way as they lost their father to alcohol. That was the day he decided to face his failure and take action. It was time to practice what he had always preached.

Abuelito was ready to make a change, but alcoholism is not something one can overcome with a snap of the fingers. Dealing with his alcoholism required consistent resilience on his end. He received the help he needed. He ditched the friends who would consistently lead him toward temptation, and he focused on being the father he always hoped to be. He told me it was one of his hardest failures, as he not only let those around him down, but himself as well. He fought and proved to himself that alcohol was not going to ruin his life. Living through that obstacle helped him become the resilient cheerleader I knew him to be.

Anytime I was personally going through a struggle or facing a failure, I would give him a call and vent. I would go on and on about a hard situation and how disappointed I was. He would kindly hear me out. When I was done, he would remind me, "Bounce back. Do not focus on how hard it is. Keep going."

Michael Jordan is another great example of obtaining the ultimate resiliency. He once admitted, "I've missed more than nine thousand shots in my career. I've lost almost three hundred games. Twenty-six times, I've been trusted to take the game winning shot and missed. I've failed over and over and over again in my life. And that is why I succeed."[42] We all know the outcomes of his multiple failures.

Unfortunately, my resilient cheerleader passed away a couple of years ago from diabetes. Until the very last minute of his life, he reminded us to keep going and be the resilient warriors he taught us to be. He wanted us to fight the fight.

Abuelito's teachings of resilience go hand-in-hand with my method of bouncing back by throwing Pity Parties. I throw Pity Parties to remind myself of my resiliency. The intention

---

42   Benjamin Hardy, "23 Michael Jordan Quotes That Will Immediately Boost Your Confidence," *Inc.*, last modified April 05, 2016.

of a Pity Party is to keep standing back up and moving forward. I know it can be scary sometimes, but do not allow fear to stop you from reaching greatness. Either face the fear and stand back up or live in regret. You decide. Your "why" needs to be so strong it anchors you down during the worst of the storm.

You are strong and can kick failure in the butt any day. If you truly want to reach success, there are no excuses. You have to work for it. Remember, nothing in life is free. Only you can decide to bounce back from adversity. You have the power to regain control of the next steps. Remember, a failure is an event. It does not define you as a person. The more comfortable you become with failure, the more resilient you will be. When you master change, you master your life. As Jim Carrey explains, "You can fail at what you don't want, so you might as well take a chance on doing what you love."[43]

Party Favors:

- STOP WASTING TIME. DO NOT DO YOURSELF A DISSERVICE BY STAYING IN FAILURE. LIFE IS TOO SHORT!
- NO MATTER HOW MANY TIMES YOU FAIL, KEEP GOING. THE MORE TIMES YOU KEEP STANDING BACK UP THE FASTER YOU WILL BECOME COMFORTABLE WITH IT. KEEP GOING!
- SUPER IMPORTANT—DO NOT GIVE UP ON YOURSELF. NO EXCUSES, STAY COMMITTED. YOU CAN DO HARD THINGS AND CAN OVERCOME ANYTHING LIFE THROWS YOUR WAY. I BELIEVE IN YOU!

---

43 Patrick Allan, "Jim Carrey on Why You Shouldn't Fear Failure," Failure, Lifehacker, last modified, July 23, 2014.

CHAPTER 5:

PITY PARTIER PRINCIPLE: NEW OPPORTUNITIES

———

"You may encounter many defeats, but you must not be defeated. In fact, it may be necessary to encounter the defeats, so you can know who you are, what you can rise from, how you can still come out of it."[44]

—*MAYA ANGELOU*

Otra oportunidad! Otra oportunidad!

When you translate *otra oportunidad* to English, it means "another opportunity." Failure is another opportunity to try again.

---

44 "Quotes On Failure (And Overcoming It) From Women Who've Succeeded Despite Their Hurdles," Culture, *ELLE Australia*, last modified September 25, 2016.

My family says this every time someone fails at something. In true Carrasco fashion, it is followed with a clap separating every syllable and ends with a big burst of laughter. We are an annoyingly positive family. We say this as a reminder that every failure and struggle is a new opportunity life is offering you.

I think the reason why we have a positive response to the topic of failure is because we have lived through it as a family in multiple instances. We are not perfect. Every family has their ups and downs throughout life, but we have been able to tackle it with positivity. I do not come from a privileged family. No trust fund here. I saw my parents work really hard to get to where they are now. I grew up seeing them exemplify failing, standing back up, and trying again. By sharing a piece of my family, I hope you can also see failure as a new opportunity.

I was born in Los Angeles, California. Now when I say Los Angeles, people tend to think the luxurious lifestyle of Hollywood. That is not the one I am referring to. Quite the opposite. When I say I was born in Los Angeles, I mean I was born in East LA I am talking East LA back in the late eighties and nineties, when it was filled with riots and the streets were ruled by gangs. People did not walk the streets once the sun went down for fear of being caught in the middle of a gang fight. Businesses closed early, and homes had thick black bar window protectors to prevent theft. Let's just say it was not the safest of neighborhoods.

Although East LA was no glam-land, I loved it because my dad worked so hard to get us there. My parents lived the idea of *otra oportunidad*, as they transformed obstacles into new opportunities. Both my parents were born and raised in Mexico. My dad moved to the United States when he was eighteen years old. The man was a non-English speaker, fresh out of high school and in pursuit of the ever-popular American dream. In 1979, he decided to chase his dreams. At the time, his older brother was living his American dream and encouraged my dad to come along. He applied for the visa, packed his things into one suitcase, and moved to Los Angeles, California. Upon asking him why he decided to come to the United States, he explained, "I was in search of new opportunities. I knew it was not going to be easy, but I was up for the challenge."

THE AMERICAN DREAM

Dad moved to LA not knowing the language nor the culture. He arrived to a foreign world. Although it was intimidating, he had audacious dreams. He promised himself no matter what got in his way, he was going to make it. Upon arriving, his older brother, who was a contractor at the time, took him under his wing. He provided him his first job as a painter. The twist here is he actually was not certified and didn't know how to paint. However, he wasn't in a position to deny any help as money was scarce. He reminisced about beginning his job and said, "I did not know anything about paint or the technique. I rolled up my sleeves and learned by watching my coworkers and asking questions."

Being a part of our family didn't mean the job was secure. No freebies were allowed. My dad had to earn his spot on the team through hard work and a willingness to learn. Whenever a misstep presented itself, he took it as a new opportunity to master his art. He studied the products they used. Weekends were dedicated to practicing his painting techniques. It was not easy, but he was determined. Dad explained, "I wanted what my brother had, my own company and being my own boss. If he did it, I knew I could too."

After living in LA for a few months, he realized not speaking the language was a disservice to his success. He had arrived with a very limited amount of money and quickly realized English classes were out of his allotted budget. He had to come up with a Plan B to learn the language. He was not going to give up his dreams just because he couldn't speak English.

He brainstormed his options. "Music", he thought. Vinyls cost a few cents, artists sang in English, and lyrics were included within the packaging. Genius! This meant he could listen to the vinyl, read along with the lyrics, and slowly start picking up on the pronunciation and spelling of words. He borrowed his brother's record player, went to his nearest record store, and bought his first set of professors: The Beatles.

My dad spent hours listening to the record. He would listen to the songs, practice his pronunciation, and search the meaning of words in his Spanish-to-English dictionary. Slowly but surely, he was able to pick up a couple of new words, which turned into small sentences. He began to teach himself English with the help of a library book. He practiced and listened to the vinyl over and over because he "did not have any other option as that was all I could afford. I created my own classroom."

Although he was not fluent, he was determined to become an owner of a company. After a couple of months, he realized that if he was going to make his dream a reality, he had to be his own boss. He recognized he needed to learn English more quickly and decided he should take classes, but he didn't have time to take them with work. The solution was to take classes and obtain projects on his own to pay for them. Dad took a leap of faith. He left his brother's company and went on his own. He really took the bull by the horns. We do have to remember laws back then were much more flexible than they are now. He did not have a painter's license at the time, but that was not an obstacle. He searched for painting jobs with surrounding homeowners and businesses.

He struggled to find projects on his own. Since he did not speak English very well, many people turned him away. He was determined to take every "no" he came across and turn it into a "yes." One day he came across a small property management company in-need of a painter. Dad was ecstatic and immediately took it. He would go to school in the morning and then hop over to work. Due to class taking up half the day, he had to make up that time by working late hours. "I remember being very tired, but it allowed me to go to school and make money at the same time," Dad recalled.

THE EXAM

After my parents got married and my brother and I were born, my dad worked even harder. After a couple of successful years painting homes in LA, he aspired to a more audacious dream in Las Vegas. He decided to move up from home painting to hotel painting. Our family packed our bags and moved to Sin City. To start working in Nevada, my dad had to take the painter's and contractor's test. My dad was one smart cookie in the business world, but studying was not his strong suit. This exam in particular was especially difficult as it included new state laws, regulations, and forgotten technicalities he had not visited in years. He struggled with new terminology. In true Dad fashion, he faced this struggle by putting all his energy into passing that test as it would open new doors for his career.

I remember seeing him pace back and forth in the kitchen, reading and marking his handbooks using a bright, neon highlighter. Any time an important item appeared in his reading he would open his orange Dunn Edwards notebook. He filled the pages with terms followed by a big asterisk to mark their importance. As exam day approached, Dad would spend all evening in the home office studying.

Exam day fell on a Tuesday. That morning, we all sat together to eat breakfast and cheered on Dad for his big day. I remember him dropping me off at school and waving goodbye to him while I yelled, "Good luck Dad! You're going to pass with flying colors!"

Upon arriving home after school, Dad sat on the living room couch. I could see tears in his eyes as I got closer. I asked, "Dad, how was the test? Did you pass?" As I stood in front of him, he looked me straight in the eyes and said, "No Dani, I failed. I let you down."

A chill ran down my spine. For the first time in my life, I heard my dad say he failed me. I could feel the disappointment emanating from his watery brown eyes. Seeing the cloud of sadness come over my dad as he sat with sloped shoulders broke my heart. That evening he gathered my brother and I and said, "Kids, I feel like I have let you two down. I did not pass my exams and feel horrible. But I want to teach you a lesson on failure. Failure is only a failure if you allow it to be. It needs to be seen as a new opportunity. I have gotten this far in life because of my failures. Do not let failures define you. Make your failures your biggest wins."

In bed that night, I kept thinking about what my dad had said:

"You need to see failure as a new opportunity."

In that moment, Webster's definition of failure was forever replaced.

The very next day, he signed up for the test again and got to work. Due to this being his second round, he knew what subjects to focus on and changed his studying technique. He learned from his initial failure how to better approach test attempt number two. The big day arrived and again, in true Carrasco manner, we cheered *otra oportunidad* as he headed to take the test again. I am happy to say the man passed. He went on to build his clientele in Las Vegas within the hospitality industry. After years of hard work, he was able to make his dream a reality. He is now the owner of a successful painting and decorating company in Las Vegas that continues to thrive year after year. I am very proud of him.

As I think about this story and everything I have experienced to this day, I am happy to say I am just like my dad. I always strive to see failures as new opportunities. I suggest you do so as well. Failure makes us reconsider, rethink, and find new avenues and strategies to achieve our goals. Failure allows you to reach your potential. As a true Pity Partier, learn from the failure and gear yourself up for the opportunity to try again. Do not allow it to hold you back. Do not give up on yourself. You are enough. Think about it this way: if you fail, the worst thing that can happen is you gain a new opportunity. You've got this! As my family would say, *otra oportunidad*!

Party Favors:

- FAILURE IS AN OPPORTUNITY TO LEARN. "FAILURE IS SIMPLY THE OPPORTUNITY TO BEGIN AGAIN, THIS TIME MORE INTELLIGENTLY."[45]—HENRY FORD
- DO NOT ALLOW YOUR EGO TO STOP YOUR GROWTH. IF YOU FALL, IT IS OKAY. YOU ARE FINE. FIND A NEW WAY TO ACHIEVE SUCCESS. AS WE LEARNED IN SHEILA'S CHAPTER, DO NOT ALLOW FAILURE TO PERSONIFY YOU.

---

45   Erika Andersen, "21 Quotes From Henry Ford On Business, Leadership And Life," *Forbes*, last modified May 31, 2013.

CHAPTER 6:

PITY PARTIER PRINCIPLE: LET IT GO

———

"You cannot control what happens to you, but you can control your attitude toward what happens to you, and in that, you will be mastering change rather than allowing it to master you."[46]

—BRIAN TRACY

I made a huge mistake that cost a non-profit fifty thousand dollars of lost revenue. It was solely my fault.

A principle I have learned through the falls and bruises my failures have provided is that I need to stop worrying about the things I cannot control. We cannot control everything life throws our way, and that is okay. The control freaks out there probably do not want to hear this, but it is true. Life

———

46 Brian Tracy Quotes, BrainyQuote.com, BrainyMedia Inc, accessed April 23, 2020.

does not ask for permission when it throws detours into our lane. I wish it did, but it doesn't work that way. I believe this is a difficult concept for some people to accept. We may not be able to control certain things in life, but we are able to control how we react to them. I know, easier said than done. I learned this the hard way earlier in my career.

During my event planner days at the non-profit St. Jude Children's Research Hospital, I was in charge of the Oklahoma City 5k Give Thanks Walk. This walk was part of a national event that took place on the same day in over thirty cities around the United States. The walks were a big deal. Everyone from upper management had their eyes on the event, particularly the founder's daughter who spearheaded all the efforts. The walks were promoted on national television on NBC's *The Today Show*. Billboards were put up on major streets, and posters were plastered around each city hosting a walk. Needless to say, I had a massive amount of pressure on my shoulders to execute a successful event.

Not only did I have the entire company's eyes on this event, but it was my time to shine as event lead. This meant my manager had given me her full trust to lead, execute, and deliver an exceptional result. No big deal, right?

In front of my colleagues my face lit up with the excitement about a new project that would highlight my skills, but internally I was stressed. I had never planned a 5k walk by myself. I remember thinking my manager had lost her mind for giving a twenty-two-year-old girl the responsibility of executing a national event of that magnitude. I had no idea what I was doing but was determined to figure it out and give it my all.

The event was no walk in the park. The planning timeline began six months out with over seventy logistical items that had to be completed within deadlines to ensure everything was up to code internally and externally. This process consisted of seemingly endless amounts of meetings with area directors, and the marketing and legal teams. There was so much pressure that my anxiety heightened in anticipation of every meeting. Before each meeting I would mentally prepare for what I was about to step into. I would close my office door, sit in my chair, face the wall, and give myself this pep talk:

"Daniela, you've got this. I know you want to quit, but you are not a quitter. You've got this!"

Due to being a team lead, my weekly one-to-one meetings with my manager would last for what felt like a lifetime. They were eternal because it required us to extensively review every little detail. Once they were over, I would drop off my paragraphs of notes in my office, grab my car keys, and head straight to the nearest Target with my work bestie, Meg. I remember leaving those meetings with a head full of anxiety, my stomach in knots, and my palms soaked with nervous sweat. Do you ever need to do a brain dump because your brain is too full of "to-do's?" I needed to do something to keep my sanity, and Target was my saving grace. Meg and I wouldn't buy anything; we'd walk the entire store and forget about work for a bit.

Although I was stressed, everything was going according to plan. I was working my butt off. I successfully booked the venue, vendors, over fifty volunteers, entertainment, and sponsorship. My event t-shirts, bags, and banners were sent to the printer. By the time September hit, the event logistics were complete. *Look at me go* I thought to myself.

During the time leading up to the walk, participants were encouraged to fundraise and many put in all of their efforts to do so. I even received an email from the top fundraising team in Kansas stating that their entire family was going to travel from different parts of the state to Oklahoma City to be part of the event. I was excited and so were the participants. The event was planned, the donations were flowing in, and suddenly so was the snow and sleet.

LOOK AT ME GO. MORE LIKE LOOK AT IT SNOW.
The week of the event, Oklahoma City was hit with a cold front. Due to the weather conditions, the walk was at risk of being canceled. Thursday prior to the walk, I woke up to a white blanket of snow outside of my window. It took me about forty minutes to clean my windshield and get it de-iced. As I drove ten miles per hour to work and slid twice in route to the office, I thought *there is no way this event could take place.* I had to cancel it.

I arrived at the office to emails from vendors suggesting the possibility of cancellation as their staff would be unable to get to the event Saturday morning. Although all signs were pointing to cancellation, upper management, which is located outside the state of Oklahoma, requested I continue as planned.

Friday arrived and Oklahoma City might as well have been the home of *Frozen*. Everything was covered in snow. The roads were not plowed, the news requested no one leave their home, and the city shut down. I promptly emailed the head of the program in upper management and demanded they let me cancel the event. There was no way the participants or I were going to be able to safely make it to the venue. As I sent my email, my inbox flooded with every vendor cancelling. I knew I was making the right choice. Unfortunately, when you work in a large organization, you have to wait for the request to go all the way up the ladder and come all the way down for you to take any official action. Corporate life: you've got to love it.

I received my cancellation approval at 4 p.m., less than twenty-four hours from what would have been the start of the event. I went full-on beast mode, sending all of the cancellation emails, changing event statuses on social media, and alerting committee members. I had so many people to contact that I didn't finish working until after 11 p.m. I shut off my laptop, sat on my couch, and the tears came rolling down. I had been given the opportunity to show what I was capable of doing, and I had failed.

I felt so stupid. The walk had my name on it, with "cancelled" in big red letters written across it. I felt defeated. I had cost the company fifty thousand dollars of unrecoverable cost. That itself killed me. The logical part of my brain understood I could not control the weather, but I still felt the despair of failure deep in my bones. I was given the opportunity to shine and I was unable to deliver.

I slept a mere two hours that night, woke up at four in the morning, and headed to the venue. Since the event was no longer taking place, I had to clear the entire course. I arrived to an eerily quiet and empty venue populated with green and white balloons and banners with the happy faces of the St. Jude children. I stood underneath the balloon arch marking the starting line for a good five minutes and imagined what it would have been like to see all of my hard work come to fruition. What it would have felt like. What it would have sounded like to have more than three hundred walkers on that course. That is something I will never know. My goals were right in front of me, yet so very far away. I had been so close to achieving my next mark, but I never did.

THE BACKLASH AND THE RESULTING PITY PARTY

The balloons were popped, the banners came down, and the venue was left bare. Just when I thought the take-down was going to be the worst part, the hate-mail came rolling in.

It turns out many participants had faced the storm and driven down to Oklahoma City to attend the walk. I received about one hundred emails from disappointed and angry participants. Some were nice about it, but others were not. One statement in particular I clearly remember read, "A good event planner would face a few inches of snow. You should quit your job."

I laugh about it now, but I remember being torn after being bullied and humiliated. My ego definitely took a hit that day. People can be severely cruel through a screen.

I went home, changed into my comfy pajamas, and the Pity Parties began. I cried, ate ice cream, devoured an entire frozen pizza, and watched sad movies. All I kept thinking about was how all of my hard work had gone to waste and the failure of not being able to deliver. Like many of us would, I blamed myself. The "woulda-coulda-shoulda" thoughts came rolling in. I took the cancellation very personally. My mind kept going back and forth with regret for not cancelling earlier. I beat myself up for it.

By Sunday evening my tears had dried and I had devoured all the ice cream my stomach could handle. It was time to wrap up that Pity Party and move forward. I failed at one event. However, I had about fifteen events on the horizon. I could not give up. The show had to go on.

I debriefed the unfulfilled event and listed every lesson I learned from this experience—cancellation plans, communication outlets, best practices, and so on. As I was doing this activity, I had the news on. In a true Oklahoma fashion, the meteorologist was on the air talking about the latest forecast. As I was reading my list, he said, "I cannot control the weather. It's my job to deliver the forecast each week, but sometimes I'm right and other times I'm wrong. I'm human."

It clicked. I'm human, and I cannot control everything! The only thing I can control is how I react to failure. That was it! Just like the meteorologist, I could not control the weather. There was nothing I could have done to avoid the snow or road closures. I also could not control the fact that I did not have the authority to cancel the event without the approval of upper management. I could either continue blaming myself or I could accept the circumstances, learn from it, see the bright side of the situation, and realize there will be things outside of my control.

We all have times in our lives when failure is caused by something outside of our control—not obtaining the promotion, missing a flight, loss of business, and so on. Do not dwell on the situation. Keep it moving! Instead, focus on what you can control: your reaction, your feelings, and your attitude. Charles R. Swindoll said it best: "Life is 10 percent what happens to you and 90 percent how you react."[47]

Remember, you cannot force things to go your way. You will be much more effective by focusing on things you can control. Getting stuck on replaying conversations or scenes does not necessarily help the situation. Instead, I suggest identifying the root cause of your fear. Why are you trying to take control and what fear are you attempting to avoid? Is the fear actually valid or are you making up a tragic outcome? Craft your own path and make the most out of each situation. Learn from the hardship.

Party Favors:

WHEN YOU COME ACROSS FAILURE DUE TO AN UNFORESEEN CIRCUMSTANCE, ASK YOURSELF:

- WHAT CAN I ACTUALLY CONTROL RIGHT NOW?
- WAS THERE ANYTHING I COULD HAVE DONE DIFFERENTLY?
- WAS I ABLE TO CONTROL THE RESULT?

If the answer is no, then you need to learn from the situation and move on. Again, let it go and keep moving forward. Do not put your time and energy into the wrong places.

---

47   "Life Is 10% What Happens To You And 90% How You React," Wanderlust Worker, accessed April 23. 2020.

CHAPTER 7:

PITY PARTIER PRINCIPLE: GRATITUDE

———

"Be thankful for what you have; you'll end up having more. If you concentrate on what you don't have, you will never, ever have enough."[48]

—*OPRAH WINFREY*

When you experience failure or a traumatic event, it is so easy to cling to the negative thoughts and emotions. We dwell on what went wrong and fixate on the failure that occurred. Stop it. The beauty around you is hard to see when your life is immersed in the shadows of failure, but that is when you need it most. Gratitude is the ray of sunshine in the midst of a storm.

---

48 The Global Eagles, "Oprah's Gratitude Journal Oprah's Lifeclass Oprah Winfrey Network," October 26, 2013, video, 3:38.

1. I am thankful for the funny GIF my coworker Bianca shared with me.
2. I am thankful for the caramel-infused coffee I had this morning.
3. I am thankful for that person who let me merge into the left lane while driving downtown during rush hour.

Welcome to my daily gratitude practice. I firmly believe gratitude is a way of life and a principle of a Pity Partier.

Now, I know some of you may be thinking there is no way thinking about something you are thankful for is going to change your mood or turn around a bad day. Trust me, I was right there with you. I rolled my eyes when I first heard of a gratitude practice. I honestly thought it was annoying and useless. I remember seeing a gratitude journal at Office Depot and thinking *who would buy such a thing?* I did not understand the concept and frankly saw it as a lie. That is, until a three-year-old cancer patient helped change my mindset and show gratitude as a way of life.

My first "big girl" job was at the happiest place on earth. No, I am not talking about Disneyland. I'm referring to the St. Jude Children's Research Hospital in Memphis, Tennessee that helps children with cancer and other catastrophic diseases. The hospital provides families with treatments, lodging, and meals at no cost. The families at St. Jude never receive a bill because the only thing the staff wants families to worry about is taking care of their child. The hospital is like no other. Upon arriving and walking through the big red-trimmed sliding doors, visitors are greeted with walls covered in art such as colorful trees, smiley faces, butterflies, and cheerful children. As they look around, smiling children are being pulled in red wagons while a pole from which hangs an IV bag, tubes, and pump trails behind. Cancer is not fun, but St. Jude attempts to keep the lives of the kids as normal as possible.

The particularly fresh air in the facility is most noticeable to visitors. Although St. Jude is a hospital, it does not smell like one. Many people are confused because the atmosphere seems like a bit of an oxymoron compared to what a hospital treating children with cancer may look or smell like. Every staff member greets patients and guests with a big genuine smile and instantly makes them feel like they are at home. The hospital staff hosts cooking events in the cafe, concerts in the courtyard (featuring celebrities when they are in town), and game nights. Trust me when I say Disneyland has nothing on them.

During my time at St. Jude, I was a bilingual regional development representative. I traveled about 70 percent of the time around the United States to raise funds for the hospital by planning elaborate events such as radiothons, 5k walks, galas, and national campaigns with sponsors. I absolutely loved working at St. Jude because it was a rewarding job. Every dollar I raised gave the babies with cancer another day of life by providing the treatments they needed. Every long night, ounce of sweat, and dose of stress was worth it. Seeing the babies go from being admitted to the hospital to being thrown the "No Mo Chemo Remission Party" made my hard work even more magical.

As rewarding as it was, St. Jude has been my hardest job to date. Only true warriors work at St. Jude. Now, I am not just saying that to pat myself on the back. No other job has worked me as hard nor challenged me mentally, emotionally, and physically as much as my role at St. Jude. Every day I had the St. Jude families in mind. They were counting on me to excel at everything I did to obtain revenue and keep the mission of the hospital, and their children, alive. This being said, failing at St. Jude was devastating. I had failed at other jobs before, and though it was sad, it wasn't heartbreaking. Failing at an event meant no donations, which meant I had children's chemo treatments on the line. It is one thing to not meet a deadline or perhaps not make a sale at work, but it is completely different when we talk about taking away a specific treatment which helps save kids' lives. Let that sink in.

Since St. Jude was my first job out of college, my initial year was chaos. I did not know how to handle stress or failure in a professional setting. College never taught that. I was taught to be successful and obtain goals. Dealing with failure was a hard lesson to learn. I would eat my feelings and get into Godzilla-like moods. It was not pretty. I would let failure take over and dig myself into a hole. That is until I met Estevan, a St. Jude patient who I will forever carry in my heart.

At the age of three, Estevan was diagnosed with acute lymphoblastic leukemia (ALL). As St. Jude states, ALL is a cancer in the blood that affects white blood cells and is the most common childhood cancer.[49] Estevan's mom explained that he was your typical three-year-old little boy who enjoyed playing hide-and-seek and bumper cars. One day Estevan told his mom he

---

49   "Acute Lymphoblastic Leukemia (ALL)," St. Jude Children's Research Hospital, accessed April 25, 2020.

had a tummy ache. Estevan's mom brushed it off because she thought he had eaten too much or too quickly. The discomfort continued the next day and the day after. Concerned about the continuous pain, Estevan's mom took him to see the doctor. Tests were instantly done, and the unfortunate news was given. Fortunately for Estevan, his doctor was aware of St. Jude and instantly referred him. Estevan was admitted to St. Jude Children's Research Hospital, and the chemo treatments began.

His rigorous treatment inhibited him from going home. When I met Estevan, he was going into his third month at St. Jude. Imagine being three years old, living in a hospital and unable to run around a park due to a fragile immune system. Not being able to play at all because you're too tired from the radiation. Although it may seem hard to believe, Estevan was the sweetest and happiest little guy. I loved him because he consistently had a huge smile on his little face.

As I walked the hallways one morning, I ran into him and his mom giggling and holding hands while skipping. They looked at each other with soft eyes full of love. Their giggles were loud and full of joyous emotion. I remember wondering how they could be so happy with everything they were going through. I stopped to say hello. Estevan's mom mentioned that they'd had a rough night as the side effects of chemo kicked in.

"We barely slept last night, but here we are enjoying our morning skip to the mailroom."

"You are such a brave and strong mom. How do you do it?" I asked.

She looked down at Estevan, softly placed her hand on his little head with small patches of thinning hair, and responded,

"We practice gratitude. We look for the small moments that make us happy and are grateful for another day together."

"Mailroom skip," Estevan said excitedly with two little jumps.

Estevan's mom continued to explain their morning ritual. "We get up, say a little prayer, and look for one thing we are both grateful for. Mailroom skip always wins."

At St. Jude, the mailroom is where patient families receive mail from their loved ones and volunteers. Uplifting letters and drawings are delivered to the families to brighten their day. Estevan was a huge fan of this. He loved receiving letters as they were small doses of encouragement. According to his mom, those letters were their fuel to continue the battle.

This three-year-old was going through one of the toughest experiences a child his age could face, yet he gained his fuel through the practice of gratitude. That got me thinking about the power of being grateful and the importance of intentionally practicing. The ability to consciously seek out the things you are thankful for in the midst of living your lowest lows. Cultivating gratitude can be incredibly powerful and beneficial.

Integrative family physician Tanmeet Sethi asserts that gratitude goes beyond the two words "thank you." In her *Ted Talk;*

Two Words That Can Change Your Life, she explains that neuroscientists from UCLA and the University of Montreal found that gratitude can work as an antidepressant by increasing the levels of dopamine and serotonin in our brains, which are the chemicals that make us happier and fuel the desire to connect with others.[50] Tanmeet also shared that in a study done by USC's Brain and Creativity Institute, practicing gratitude stimulates the same parts of our prefrontal cortex that light up on a MRI when our pain decreases while we are with someone we love."[51]

Tanmeet Sethi further attests, "Gratitude fundamentally changes our relationship toward pain. When we say thank you to our pain, we remove our resistance and that space can be filled with joy."[52]

After meeting Estevan and being skeptical of this whole thing, I gave it a try. At the end of the day, I had nothing to lose. I made gratitude a part of my daily routine. Every day I searched and acknowledged things I was grateful for. I appreciated every good thing in my life and discovered there was nothing too small to not be thankful for. I began with little things such as being thankful for my morning coffee. I know it may sound silly, but I found myself changing my mindset to be happier and much more optimistic. I got in the habit of searching for what I refer to as "happy nuggets" throughout the day. Even when experiencing a bad day at work, my gratitude helped me to stay grounded. It allowed me to see the bigger picture of the situation and feel thankful

---

50 *TEDx Talks*, "Two Words That Can Change Your Life | Tanmeet Sethi | TEDxRainier," February 16, 2017, video, 16:47.

51 *TEDxTalks*, "Two Words That Can."

52 *TEDxTalks*, "Two Words That Can."

for all the other little things that went right during the day. We are often so busy reacting to what life throws our way that we rarely stop and smell the roses. Everyone's days are consistently filled with "happy nuggets," and you need to take a moment to acknowledge them.

My gratitude practice is now a daily routine. Every day I write down three things I am grateful for. I think this has helped me to become more positive and not allow negative emotions to fully take over. The ability to pause during a failure or pain and find one thing to be thankful for is important. Train your gratitude muscle. The more you intentionally look for the good things in life, the more they will be present in your life.

Party Favors:

How to incorporate gratitude into your daily life:

- START BY **FINDING ONE THING EVERY DAY** YOU ARE THANKFUL FOR AND WRITE OR TYPE IT IN YOUR NOTES.
- THINK ABOUT **ONE THING YOU CAN BE EXCITED** FOR BEFORE STARTING YOU DAY. DO NOT OVERTHINK THIS ONE. THIS CAN BE SOMETHING SMALL.
- **START A GRATITUDE JAR**—EVERY DAY DROP A DAILY GRATITUDE NOTE INTO A JAR. WHENEVER YOU ARE IN NEED OF A PICK-ME-UP, TAKE OUT A NOTE AND READ IT OUT LOUD.
- **SEND A THANK YOU NOTE TO A FRIEND OR COLLEAGUE**— WE CAN ALL BE MUCH MORE VOCAL ABOUT THANKING PEOPLE. YOU WILL NOT ONLY MAKE SOMEONE'S DAY A LITTLE BRIGHTER, BUT YOU WILL ALSO FEEL GREAT.
- **VOLUNTEER**—MAKE TIME TO HELP OTHERS.

CHAPTER 8:

PITY PARTIER PRINCIPLE: CONFIDENCE

———

"I have not failed 10,000 times. I have not failed once. I have succeeded in proving that those 10,000 ways will not work. When I have eliminated the ways that will not work, I will find the way that will work."[53]

—THOMAS EDISON

I thrive on rejection. I welcome it with open arms and a hug. The reason I feel this way is because I firmly believe builds confidence.

Before we get into the details, I want to touch on this subject because failures and resiliency come with a side of rejection. Throughout this book, I promote displaying resiliency through trying again and not giving up after experiencing

---

53   R.L. Adams, "21 Famous Failures Who Refused to Give Up," HUFFPOST, last modified September 16, 2017.

failure. However, as you stand back up and become resilient warriors, you will be met with rejection. I can cheer you on and give you an uplifting pep talk, but I want to ensure you are prepared to receive rejection because it can be an ego boost.

I hate to break it to you, but rejection makes a handful of appearance throughout life. Rejection is experienced in school when the popular kids didn't let you into their group. Perhaps the person you had a crush on decided to date someone else. Maybe that promotion at work does not work out. No matter how it is experienced, we can all agree it sucks and hurts. According to a Purdue Study, social rejection activates many of the same brain regions involved in physical pain.[54] For most people, the pain of rejection is something they work to avoid at all costs.

Everyone reacts to being turned down differently. We all know one person who reacts to rejection with the typical "F-that" or "I didn't really like that place or person anyway." They are in denial of the rejection. Rejection debilitates some people. For others, it strengthens and even motivates them. What is their key component? Confidence is the key component.

A study conducted by Cornell and Johns Hopkins University found that if you can proceed in a positive way, rejection can actually bolster your creativity.[55] Being rejected consistently

---

54   Kirsten Weir, "The Pain Of Social Rejection," *Monitor on Psychology* 43, no. 4(2012): 50.

55   Patrick Ercolano, "Don't Get Mad, Get Creative: Social Rejection Can Fuel Imagination, JHUCarey Researcher Finds." Johns Hopkins University, last modified August 21, 2012.

throughout my career is what has taught me to love it so much and convert those negative feelings into confidence. I trained myself to make it work in my favor. All of the falls, bruises, and tears taught me to let go of expectations of perfection and be comfortable with failure.

THANK YOU, NEXT.

Upon arriving in Seattle and being laid off from the telecommunications company, I was back on the job market. At the time, I did not understand why everything had happened. I even thought the whole thing was a sign that moving to Seattle had been a mistake. Either way, I had to get back into the game and find a job. I could not allow one setback to keep me down. Pity Partiers know better. It was time to stop whining and take action. As per usual, I threw myself a Pity Party to gear up for the next step.

I was ready to makes moves. I turned on my outdated Apple laptop, opened Google, and began the job search. I opened my resume and began to update it by typing, "Customer Success Manger (March 2017–May 2017)." Oh, the agony.

That small line of text plastered on the very top of my resume instantly made me very self-conscious. I was convinced the short amount of time spent at my most recent position would lead recruiters to assume the worst. Perhaps they would think I was fired for all the wrong reasons. Maybe, they would view it as me being unable to sustain a job. So many scenarios ran through my head. In reality, it was my ego talking as my fears manifested. Our doubts are not the truth. I caught myself, shut those thoughts down, and got to work. I knew my potential and was certain I would kick ass anywhere I got my foot in the door. I set out to find myself my next big position.

After a good two days of doing research on companies and playing *Carmen San Diego*, the infamous animated spy cartoon, I found a job posting which caught my interest. It had my name written all over it. The position was a customer-focused role within Amazon. I had the experience they were seeking and more. I was confident and knew it was going to be mine. I uploaded my resume, cover letter, filled in more than forty fields every job site requires, and sent in my application for review.

If there is one lesson my parents have taught it is to never put all of my eggs into one basket. Therefore, even though I felt like the Amazon opportunity was guaranteed, I continued to apply to other positions. By my tenth application, I had written down my address and job history so many times it all became a blur. One of the reasons I strongly dislike job hunting is because companies will ask you to upload your resume and then require you to practically copy everything you just uploaded into their own fields. It makes no sense. Gah, the frustration! I persevered and completed as many applications as possible. The post-application anticipation began.

I am not obsessed with my phone. In fact, I am actually very detached from it. However, once applications went out, I had a paper and glue relationship with it. I was consistently refreshing my emails every ten minutes and freaked out every time my phone rang. My life centered around my phone. I would even test call my friends just to make sure my phone was working correctly. The things we do when we are in a vulnerable state.

One sunny jobless morning I was sipping coffee in the kitchen and my phone alerted me to a new email. I opened it to discover it was an email from the Amazon HR. I instantly opened it and read:

"Dear Daniela,

Thank you for applying. We'd like to set up an interview within the next couple of days with one of our HR managers. Please reply with your availability."

I responded immediately and began prepping for the interview. This was it. I was already imagining myself in Bezosland. *Wow, how great would it be to work for Amazon* I thought. I researched everything from Jeff Bezos, to their company values, to the hiring manager. I might as well have applied for the FBI because I found every piece of information possible. I was ready to make this job mine.

The interview questions were fairly standard: tell me about yourself, why did you leave your past company, why Amazon, what has been your greatest accomplishment, and so on. After talking about myself for a good ten minutes, the manager explained a bit more about the position, I asked questions, and it was over. I was told I would hear back from them within the week. I felt good about the conversation and confident I was going to obtain a second interview.

After the Amazon interview came three other companies. I would go through the same emotional rollercoaster with each interview—the prep, the nerves, giving the same spiel over and over. I thought dating was tough, but interviews are their own beasts. You have a ten to fifteen minutes to make yourself shine, but you have to be careful not to sound too cocky, yet still be friendly and professional.

Two weeks went by and rejection came knocking at my front door. Amazon was the first to send the classic rejection email that said something like, "Thank you for applying. Unfortunately, at this time we have decided to move forward with another candidate. We wish you the best on your future endeavors." I was bummed, but I moved past it.

After Amazon, others followed. Job rejections are the absolute worst, and many times you never learn the details of why they said no. You begin to over-analyze yourself. You start to pick apart everything from your tone to your answers. I began to dread my email notifications and the impending rejections.

I was getting frustrated and my ego was at a level two. How was I supposed to show recruiters my best version when I had been stomped on by every other employer? I felt like a beat-up piñata at a children's birthday party. Thrashed at every angle yet attempting to hold itself together by one string. I couldn't take it anymore after I read the sixth rejection. I was failing at every single job had I applied for.

That was my queue to throw a Pity Party. I went to the gym and exercised the frustration out of my system by using the

StairMaster. Whenever I am feeling frustrated, this piece of gym equipment is my hero because that machine is the embodiment of Satan. One minute you are breathing as a human should, and the next you feel like you just ran a marathon with weights. However, once you conquer it, it makes you feel like a million bucks. So if you ever see me on a StairMaster, do not bug me. You've been warned.

After the gym, I called the pep-talk master, my best friend Meg. Meg and I met when we both worked at St. Jude Children's Research Hospital. We experienced some of the toughest moments in our careers together in that position. Therefore, when one of us is going through a rough time we know exactly what to say to each other to remind ourselves we have been through harder things and survived. I vented to her about my applications, interviews, and rejections. I am sure the poor girl was praying someone would hire me so my venting and long call sessions would end.

Meg advised, "You have been through this before and survived. Do not give up. Just know you are not going to be jobless forever. You just have not found the right job for you. Learn from every "no" and focus."

After a couple of weeks, I was invited to an in-person interview at a company that creates apps. I arrived at the office and spoke with the team lead. Following the team lead, I was to be interviewed by the department manager, but to my surprise the HR manager arrived instead. She said there had been a change in schedule and I was being sent home. I was confused and startled. Did my first interview go so badly it made them cancel the day-long interview? As she began to explain, I realized I was getting sent home with one of the biggest lessons I'll ever learn in life.

REJECTION LEADS TO SUCCESS AND CONFIDENCE

I was told the team felt the position I applied for was not going to be enough of a challenge for me. They saw something bigger in my future, and they did not want to stand in the way.

"It may not feel like it now, but we hope this rejection makes you stronger. Do not sell yourself short. There are bigger, better things coming your way," explained the HR manager.

All I could think at the moment was *are you kidding me?* I was annoyed and confused with the process. I grabbed my purse and was escorted out. Walking home, I replayed her message over and over again. I did not understand how rejection was supposed to make me stronger. I was exhausted and hanging on by a thread. I took the rest of the day off to think about my next step.

I had been applying and interviewing, but I haven't gotten anywhere. I suddenly pieced everything together. Although I was being rejected over and over again, I kept going. It sucked and did not feel good, but what other option did I have? Giving up was not going to be the solution. My mama did not raise a quitter. Perhaps she was right. Each "no" was making me stronger for the future. Every time I received a rejection letter, I would go back and assess the event. I created a list of items I could improve on such as my responses, my questions, and the layout of my resume. Doing that practice, I quickly realized I was selling myself short. I was applying for jobs for which I was overqualified. As author Steve Maraboli explains, "As I look back on my life, I realize that every time I thought I was being rejected from something good, I was actually being redirected to something better."[56]

Every rejection helped me become more confident. By the time in-person interviews came along, I would walk into those offices with my head held high and ready to show the employer why I deserved the position. I actually switched the roles. I began to interview the companies instead of the other way around. I wanted to know why I should give the company my talent. I knew my worth.

I began to change my view toward rejection. As it appeared, I became more confident. I would say to myself, "That is okay. That job was not meant to be." One door closes and two others open. I would learn from every "no". I would pat myself on the back for trying. I kept up my spirits. Two months into unemployment, the sun began to shine. I received offer letters from various companies. I was down to two when suddenly a new opportunity came knocking on my door. I received a message via LinkedIn. The message was from a marketing director stating they were interested in speaking with me because they thought I would be a good fit for their team. It was another startup.

At this point in my life I was traumatized with startups. I could not possibly take another risk again. I was determined

---

56 Steve Maraboli, "You're Not Rejected – You're Redirected," Steve Maraboli, accessed on May 25, 2020.

to stay safe and go work for a large corporation. However, my gut urged me to respond to the message and give it a try. That was the day Knock came into my life.

Knock, a company specializing in customer-relationship management for residential property management companies based in Seattle, was just five years old with a team of about ten people. I went in to the in-person interview with no hopes of it working out. I decided to go and meet the team to learn about the company, but I was determined to turn down the offer. Little did I know that every rejection I had faced for the past two plus months would lead to my biggest win.

I met with the team and felt at home within the first hour. The product was very intriguing, the staff was awesome, and the challenge was vast. It was just what I was looking for. I walked out of the office knowing it was my new home.

Three years later, and I call Seattle home because of this company. If it were not for Knock, I would have left Seattle a long time ago. The way life works is funny. It may be difficult for us to see and understand the bigger picture while living within our failure. However, I truly believe every rejection is building us up to become more confident with ourselves and leading us to our next big step. If I would had not experienced rejection, I may never have gained all of these opportunities.

Do not dwell on the rejection. Confidence means letting it sting for a bit, recognizing the feelings, and converting them into knowledge and power. By practicing this, you will gain a growth mindset. Carol Dweck, lead researcher in the field of motivation, describes a "growth mindset" as a mindset which allows you to think your abilities can improve, and a challenge is an opportunity to learn and grow.[57] Do not take rejection personally. I hate to burst your bubble, but it is not always about you. Do not associate rejection with personal value or sense of worth. Instead, let your rejections be proof you are pushing yourself outside of your boundaries and comfort zone, just like Thomas Edison did. Although he holds 1093 patents, he failed over ten thousand times upon his invention of a commercially-viable electric light bulb.[58]

Look back on your life and reflect on all the instances you have experienced rejection. I am sure you felt distraught at the time, but you are still moving forward. If you are currently experiencing rejection, embrace it and build self-confidence. I understand it is easier said than done. Hear me when I say to not give up, and keep pushing through because you are on the road to your magical ending.

Upon asking my pep talk master for a couple of words of advice on this topic, Meg said, "The worst thing you can do is continuously beat yourself up. The most important thing to do is to identify the lesson, let yourself feel it, and move on. Don't stay in it. You're better than that." The path is not easy, but take every rejection as a confidence booster. Every time you fall, throw yourself a Pity Party, and stand up again with even more confidence than before. You are strong and can achieve anything life throws your way.

---

57   Angelica Florio, "Need a Confidence Boost? Try Failing.," Next Big Idea Club, last modified December 08, 2015.

58   R.L. Adams, "21 Famous Failures Who Refused to Give Up," HUFFPOST, last modified September 16, 2017.

> "Become so confident in who you are that no one's behavior, opinion, or rejection can affect you."[59]

—BRAD TURNBULL

Remember, failure molds you into the person you were meant to be.

Party Favors:

HOW TO CONVERT REJECTION TO CONFIDENCE:

- ALLOW YOURSELF TO FEEL THE STING. DO NOT SUPPRESS YOUR FEELINGS BECAUSE IT IS WORSE TO BOTTLE THINGS UP. IF YOU WANT TO CRY, GRAB THE TISSUES. IF YOU WANT TO LET OUT SOME STREAM, GO TO THE GYM. REJECTION IS NOT FUN—ALLOW YOURSELF TO FEEL THE FEELINGS.
- LEARN, LEARN, LEARN. CREATE AN ASSESSMENT OF THE REJECTION AND LEARN FROM IT.
- CELEBRATE YOUR EFFORT. GIVE YOURSELF PROPS FOR TRYING.
- BE READY FOR THE "NO'S." REJECTION IS PART OF LIFE. INSTEAD OF REACTING, BE READY TO RESPOND TO REJECTION.
- TREAT YOURSELF WITH COMPASSION. NEGATIVE SELF-TALK HELPS NO ONE. BE GENTLE WITH YOURSELF.

---

59 Brad Turbull, "Inspirational Quotes," The Mindset Journey, last modified June 07, 2017.

CHAPTER 9:

PITY PARTIER 101

———

"Now, when you're down there in the hole, it looks like failure. When that moment comes, it's okay to feel bad for a little while. Give yourself time to mourn what you think you may have lost. But then, here's the key: Learn from every mistake, because every experience, particularly your mistakes, are there to teach you and force you into being more who you are."[60]

—OPRAH WINFREY

If there is one thing I wish for you, it is failure. Failure is the key to success and the greatest win you will ever experience. The only way to reach the mountain top is one failure after the other. The time has come to get out of that comfort zone, people. Welcome to Pity Partier 101: The Step-by-Step Guide to Becoming an Effective Pity Partier.

Now before we get into learning mode, let's be honest with each other. Failure sucks. Listen, I can preach about

---

60 "Winfrey's Commencement Address," The Harvard Gazette, last modified May 31, 2013.

embracing failure all day long, but I am also realistic. I understand it is frickin' hard to get back up sometimes. I do not magically wake up to a life of rainbows and butterflies. I wish I did, because that would be awesome. I have failed and cried myself to sleep, felt embarrassed, and fearful to try again. I am consistently forced to coach myself with my Pity Party Method. Honestly, I am experiencing failure as I write this book. Funny, isn't it? I am literally living in failure even as I write about it.

Writing a book is difficult. The process has been hard, stressful, and overwhelming. It has challenged me in a way I had never been before. People say writing a book is a form of soul searching, which is true. It makes you vulnerable because you put everything out there. It has certainly pulled me out of my own comfort zone.

I have cried a good dozen times over this book. I am talking about the ugly cries from feeling overwhelmed. It has been stressful because I am continuing to work my full-time job throughout this journey. During that time, I have to put out fires at work, customers who need my full attention, and a team counting on me to put my best foot forward. After that, I worked on this book from about 7:30 p.m. until 10 p.m., and poured my heart into it and tried to avoid writer's block. I have failed to meet deadlines. I have failed to be fully present for my friends and family. I have failed at work. To say the least, failure is no stranger in this process. However, with the help of Pity Parties, I have been able to wipe my tears, pick myself up, and cheer my way to completion. With every setback, I have unleashed the lessons, created tactical plans to move toward my goals, and celebrated each small triumph. It has been hard, but I did it! I have completed each chapter, met my fundraising goal, and am on the last push toward publication. I am proud to say I am now celebrating my failures with the book you currently hold in your hands, which feels so good to type out!

Now that you've read about the various Pity Partier Principles and have a better understanding of their roots, it's time to show you how you can incorporate this method into your life. I want people to stop complaining about their failures and start taking action. You may say it is hard, or think you are not wired like I am. I do not want to hear excuses. Do not tell me you do not have it in you to want something more of your life. Wrap up the excuses, learn, and stand back up! You can either live the life you want or sit in regret forever. The Pity Party Method can be used any time a failure is experienced. It is time to throw yourself three Pity Parties and start celebrating your failures.

A good theme can transform a Pity Party into a truly fun and memorable event. I love themed parties because they get my creative juices flowing. Therefore, I present the three Pity Party Themes.

PARTY THEME ONE: FEEL THE FEELINGS.
If you want to cry, get those tissues ready. If you want to scream, get those lungs working. If you want to punch something, head to the gym and go to town on a punching bag. Whatever you are feeling, allow yourself to truly feel those emotions. I repeat—do not avoid your emotions. This is not the time to be shy or hide your feelings. If you are someone

who covers emotions with a happy hour at the bar, alcohol is not the solution here. This is the time to fully embrace your emotions. Be true to yourself. Let it out and let it be heard. A study published in the *Journal of Behavioral Decision Making* discovered that it is more beneficial to think and allow yourself to embrace your emotions rather than focusing on the failure itself.[61]

Some people may find this very simple to do while others may find it to be a challenge. Yes, I am talking to those of you who bottle up emotions and keep shoving them down—the "I'm fine-ers." If that is you, I get it. I did the same thing. I am a people pleaser and thought showing my emotions would let people down or make them uncomfortable. I did not want to be labeled as too sensitive or dramatic, and I definitely didn't want to be misjudged.

I quickly realized that instead of letting others down, I was letting down the most important person in my life: me. In the midst of failure, you matter the most. Let me repeat that for the people in the back: Do not let anyone else dictate your feelings. I would bottle so many emotions that I shut down. I was no longer myself. For those of you who do this, you need to understand hiding feelings isn't going to magically make them disappear forever. You need to realize that by bottling up emotions, your emotions will weigh you down.

Imagine every emotion being a pond rock. Each individual rock may be relatively small, but now imagine trying to carry

---

61   Noelle Nelson, Selin A. Malkoc, and Baba Shiv, "Emotions Know Best: The Advantage of Emotional versus Cognitive Responses to Failure," *Behavioral Decision Making* 31, no. 1 (January 2018): 40-51.

every rock in one hand. It would eventually get really heavy and the rocks would begin to weigh down your hand as you continued to add more. Eventually, the rocks would fall due to an inability to hold them all. This is exactly what you do when you bottle everything up. Let it go. Identify the feeling, name it, and take action.

PARTY THEME TWO: DO SOMETHING THAT MAKES YOU HAPPY.

This theme is my absolute favorite. After all, who doesn't enjoy being happy? After experiencing failure, do something that truly makes you happy. A team of psychologists from University of California Riverside found that positive emotions may help those trapped or feeling helpless in the midst of negative moods.[62]

Two things instantly make me happy: driving and showering. If I am ever in need of a happiness boost, hand me my keys and get the tunes going. Driving with no destination and a good soundtrack instantly changes my mood. My soundtrack is a Six Flags-like rollercoaster. It goes up, down, and around. I can start off with Beyoncé, move on to Adele, Disney soundtracks, and hip-hop. I allow myself to completely tune out everything I am stressing about and drive. The permission I give to myself to focus on the road, is so liberating. In addition, I perform a live karaoke session as I sing my heart out and dance in my seat.

---

62 Kristin Layous, Joseph Chancellor, and Sonja Lyubomirsky, "Positive Activities as Protective Factors Against Mental Health Conditions," *Journal of Abnormal Psychology* 123, no. 1 (2014): 3-12.

Showers are my second happy place. My friends know that if I am in a funky mood, I need to be guided to the nearest shower as soon as possible. Allowing water to wash everything away helps clear my head, change my attitude, and boosts my mood.

Your go-to happy place will most likely be different than mine. What works for me might not work for you. Your happy place may be an art class, the gym, or a trip to the mall. If you cannot identify one, think of a place or an activity that instantly gets you in a good mood or makes you smile. This should be something that allows you to be you. Do not judge yourself. Whatever it is, you need to be aware of it so you can do it after experiencing all of your feelings. Doing whatever makes you happy instantly changes your state of mind.

"Having a space that you can go to, to center and find clarity, is extremely beneficial," says Dr. Jaime Kulaga, PhD.[63] He also affirms that "When you step away to a calm space that brings you joy or peacefulness, you allow your mind to destress so that you can make clear-minded decisions and see things from alternate perspectives."[64]

After Pity Party Number One of "feeling your feelings," you may feel like a deflated balloon. You need your happy place to elevate your spirits. Do not give up on yourself. Throw on music, lace up those sneakers, do whatever you have to do to get yourself into a state of happiness.

---

63 Sarah Crow, "This Is Why You Need a "Happy Place"—and Where to Find It," Best Life, last modified October 26, 2013.

64 Sarah Crow, "This Is Why You Need a "Happy Place"—and Where to Find It," Best Life, last modified October 26, 2013.

PITY PARTY THEME THREE: GET OUT OF THE PICKLE.

Now that you are feeling pumped, it is time to find the lesson from the failure and create a game plan to move forward. This last Pity Party is where you figure out your next step. By now, you know me pretty well, so I am being transparent. Pity Party Number Three can be a bit of a struggle sometimes. The primary reason is because the little negative voice in my brain makes a special appearance. It tends to say something such as, "You are not going to be able to make it work. You are going to fail again. Do not try again. Just stay here."

I believe we all have those instances where we have an angel sitting on our right shoulder and the devil on the left. Brush that devil off and believe you can and will, and you must move forward from this situation. If you do not wholeheartedly believe in yourself, then no one else will. It does not matter how many cheerleaders you have around you or how many personal development books you read. Believe in your own strength.

Step One: Seek growth. Assess the failure and find the lessons. Learn from your mistakes. Trust me, every setback has at least one lesson that can be uncovered. Take a look at what caused the failure. Is there an identifiable root cause? What did you learn? What could you have done differently? What skills can you sharpen or learn to prevent you from failing again? Can anyone help you learn these skills? Learn to work smarter, not harder. An example of this would be the time I had to cancel the walk due to the snowstorm. After that failure, I assessed the event by asking myself:

- What did I learn? Answer: Every event must have a backup plan. I cannot cancel an event with a notice of less than twenty-four hours.
- What could I have done differently? Answer: Knowing a snowstorm was a possibility, I should have created a Plan B.
- What skills can I improve to prevent this from occurring? Answer: Sharpen my problem-solving skills as I was not prepared with the last-minute cancellation.
- Who can help me fine-tune my skills? Answer: My region's event specialist can help me as she has eleven years of experience in event planning.

Failure demonstrates our strengths and weaknesses. Find those teachable moments and identify the issues that need to be corrected when pursuing tasks or goals moving forward.

When it comes to moving forward, motivational speaker Rachel Hollis says it best in her talk on goal setting: "If you don't know where you are going, how are you going to get there? You have to have a destination in mind."[65]

Step Two: Identify your destination and your end goal. It is time to focus and put your eyes on the prize. You got kicked out of your lane, but it is time to get back on the road and continue your journey. What is your gas going to be when times get tough? This step is so important as you will use it as your anchor for when storms roll through. Whatever your goal is, visualize it, feel it, and believe it.

---

65   *Rachel Hollis*, "2020 Goal Setting | Rachel Hollis," January 14, 2020, video, 47:46.

Step Three: How will you get there? Create a game plan to get back out there and attain the goal. Put on your planning hat. Do not overthink this process. List out the steps to take to reach the end goal. I ask you to not overthink this as I believe the best ideas come during a good brainstorming session. Again, think big picture and just write everything that must be done. Breakdown the plan in chunks. Decide on the first step and, as Nike's slogan says, "Just Do It." Do not look back at the pas—look forward and onward. Remember, the third Pity Party is the last one. Do not procrastinate and, most importantly, do not give up on yourself. If that little devil's voice comes back, brush it off. You need to plan and execute.

I will use my dad's American dream of owning a home but inability to obtain a job due to the language barrier as an example. Think of the end goal and work backward. Create a small outline of the steps you need to achieve to reach your destination. For him to purchase a home, he had to get a job to earn a living. Being a non-English speaker impeded him from being hired. Since he could not afford English classes, he decided to learn with the help of vinyl records.

- Step One: Purchase a vinyl record.
- Step Two: Learn to speak English.
- Step Three: Find a job.
- Step Four: Save money.
- Step Five: Purchase a home.

> Do not overwhelm yourself. Take it step-by-step. Vision cast your goal and design your own game plan. You've got this!

I truly mean it when I say you've got this. You are intelligent and can achieve anything you set your mind to. If you have not heard this lately, I am here to remind you that you are a badass. Stop beating yourself up with negativity. Surrender those thoughts and start believing in yourself. Every failure should be celebrated to allow yourself to propel forward. Failing is not bad. If you are failing, it means you are trying and getting out of that comfort zone. No matter what failure you are currently experiencing, big or small, you can overcome it by becoming a Pity Partier. I have seen the magic and let me tell you, you will surprise yourself with the power you are holding back. I believe in you. Welcome to the party!

Party Favors:

IT IS TIME TO THROW ON THAT PARTY HAT AND CELEBRATE YOUR FAILURES!

- FEEL THE FEELINGS. LET IT OUT, MY FRIEND. HOLDING OR SUPPRESSING YOUR EMOTIONS WILL NOT HELP YOU.
- DO SOMETHING THAT CHEERS YOU UP AND MAKES YOU HAPPY: DANCE, PAINT, WORK OUT. WHATEVER BRINGS A SMILE TO YOUR FACE, DO IT!
- MAKE A GAME PLAN FOR YOUR ROAD TO SUCCESS. LINE OUT THE STEPS YOU NEED TO TAKE TO MOVE FORWARD. LEARN, PLAN, AND EXECUTE.

CHAPTER 10:

HEARTBREAK, HAPPY NEW YEAR!

———

"The most empowering part of failing is picking yourself back up. The process toward recovery is so much enjoyable than what people think! The first step is scary, but once you get through it, you realize you are going to be okay."
—KATRINA CONCEPCION, YODA LOVE EXPERT

In a book that discusses how to overcome failure, the topic of experiencing failure in love could not be skipped. As a true Pity Partier, every setback is celebrated, even if it pertains to a broken heart. Every heartbreak provides an opportunity to learn, grow, and assist you on our journey to become the best version of yourself. Breakups don't have to leave you broken.

Breakups, divorces, and the end of relationships are never fun. Relationships are no walk in the park as they require ongoing commitment, dedication, and communication. I am going to be honest—the conclusion of any relationship sucks. However, sometimes things do not work out. No one goes into a relationship thinking *I hope this does not last.* However, some relationships are meant to be seasonal. We are human, and change is inevitable. Some people are better separate rather than together.

In true Pity Partier fashion, you learn and grow from the situation. That being said, I encourage you to view breakups like a New Year's Eve celebration. You read that correctly, but hear me out. Upon approaching December 31st, people do a year-end reflection as an analysis of their life choices, figuring out what worked and what did not. After reflection come resolutions. With the motivation of the New Year, we create goals, envision adventures, and gear ourselves to meet the next twelve months with our best foot forward. This same approach is what I encourage you to practice after a relationship has failed.

Now I am not expecting people to breakup and automatically pop a bottle of champagne. If you need to grieve and take your time, please do that. As you just learned in Pity Partier 101, feeling your feelings is extremely important. According to clinical psychologist Adam Borland PsyD, "Grieving is a natural process after any kind of loss. It helps our brains adjust to our new reality. Avoiding grief can keep you stuck in feelings of sadness, loneliness, guilt, shame, and anger—which can take a big toll on your self-esteem."[66]

---

66 "Grieving After a Break-Up? 6 Strategies to Help You Heal," Metal Health, Cleveland Clinic, last modified January 23, 2019.

I know having your heart broken is painful. Ben & Jerry might as well give me company stock with the amount of ice cream I have consumed after breakups. However, after all the tears and closures, I overcame every one of them. Looking back now I can honestly say no matter how difficult; I am so thankful for every single one of them. I truly look at every ex-partner and thank them. Why? They made me stronger, more confident, and an overall better person and partner. Sometimes we have to go through bumpy roads (and lots of Half-Baked ice cream) to help us get to the beautiful scenic route. As the Yoda Love Expert says, "Every relationship has ups and downs. When it's time to exit a relationship, leave with memories of the good times and the lessons from the bad times."

YODA LOVE EXPERT WEIGHS IN

When it comes to the topic of failure experienced in love, I could not think of a better person to speak about this subject other than the funny and kind-hearted Katrina Concepcion, also known as the Yoda Love Expert, co-host of the podcast *For No Good Reason* (FNGR).

Katrina, the in-studio love expert, provides advice and techniques to maneuver through the world of love. This sweet 5'2" girl does not fall short when it comes to the topic of love. Katrina's experience is varied and broad. She has been in committed relationships, short-term relationships, catfished, and even cheated on. In our conversation over the phone, I learned more about how Katrina's biggest heartbreak led her to her greatest love conquest. "Breaking up or being broken up with means you don't have to waste another minute with someone who isn't right for you. You get to begin a new adventure," she advised.

Katrina may hold the love expert title now, but she did not always have the answers. With an abundance of love stories under her belt, Katrina attributed being cheated on by a soon-to-be fiancé as her biggest failure in love. However, a failed relationship did not correlate to failure as she considers breakups an opportunity to come back stronger and better. She explained, "There is a common stereotype when it comes to love: 'Being single is hard.' I promise that being in a loveless, toxic, or boring relationship is much harder. Singlehood is what you make it. After the breakup, don't pick apart how you could have saved that relationship. The only thing you can change... is yourself. Re-evaluate your needs and wants."

Many women growing up dream of that special day when Prince Charming kneels down, pops the question, and reveals a magnificent sparkling ring. That moment when fireworks burst in the air and the future union is celebrated. That exact scene is what Katrina was getting ready for, until her soon-to-be-engagement celebration went from a visit to a ring shop to couple's therapy.

Upon graduating college, Katrina finished dating fraternity boys. She was determined to find herself a responsible, caring, and loving man. She signed up for the latest dating apps and began the search. This resulted in meeting an array of men. After a few weeks of swiping left and right, she met Mark. Mark was different, successful, and everything those fraternity boys were not, she explained, "I let myself believe that because he was different, everything was going to be better. I thought, 'this guy is not like those other guys. That means he is special.'"

Katrina and Mark's flame ignited on Tinder. Mark was visiting from New York on a business trip to Las Vegas. They met up for coffee, and sparks flew instantly. Their chemistry was aligned, they found each other attractive, and both were in tune with what they wanted in life. Due to Mark consistently being in Las Vegas for business, they decided to move forward with the long-distance relationship. Katrina recalls Mark being the ideal man at the time: "He was perfect on paper. He was that guy society tells you to go for. He was the guy in the knit cardigan at Christmas that gave her an extraordinary gift. He had the ideal family, perfect house, nice car, and good job."

Katrina experienced a fairytale love story which consisted of lavish vacations and romantic gestures. As months passed by, the relationship progressed. He was introduced to her family and friends. Everyone instantly approved and became fans of him. Although he painted the perfect picture on the outside, Katrina felt that was not the case on the inside. Mark was perfect on paper and everyone adored him, however, she recalled feeling disconnected and she stated, "I did not feel close to him, but I ignored the feelings. I did not want to mess this up. I kept telling myself being with someone so perfect was the grown-up thing to do. Just shut up."

Katrina reviewed her love timeline:

- Meet the guy: Check.
- Fall in love: Check.
- Get engaged: Next step.

One day while Katrina was in New York visiting Mark, she had trouble sleeping due to a gut feeling. It was so strong it woke her up and led her pacing around his house. As she attempted to relax, she decided to watch some TV. She noticed a bright flash and heard a buzzing noise coming from a pile of papers in the living room. The light consistently kept flashing. She dug through the pile to discover an iPad; one Mark never expected her to find. "As I held the iPad and read the flashing notifications, my entire timeline, expectations, and everything that I thought was going to happen for me crumbled," Katrina described.

Mark was cheating.

As Katrina held the iPad and began to read the incoming notifications, she realized other women existed in his life. Fairytale love suddenly transformed into a nightmare. Katrina uncovered it all. Everything she had been living was a lie. Her hopes to be engaged and move to New York all went crumbling down. She admitted, "I remember feeling really cold, even though it wasn't. I was shaking. I was livid, shocked, and felt humiliated."

Upon confronting him, the truth was revealed. Well, at least half of it. He confessed to interacting with other women and still being active in online dating apps. Katrina felt vulnerable but, being naive, decided to give him another opportunity. They signed up for couple's therapy, and the forgiveness journey began. Unfortunately, through the process, she discovered the infidelity did not terminate. Katrina described being embarrassed to even voice the reality of the situation. She said, "Infidelity is a failure so deep that it results in you feeling insecure and unloved. It makes you feel not worthy of this person, not worthy of loyalty. It puts you in such a vulnerable spot. You blame yourself. You feel like a failure although it wasn't your fault this person failed you."

Upon reflecting on the situation, Katrina realized a diamond would not guarantee Mark's cheating would come to an end. She had lost herself by agreeing to stay in that relationship and she realized, "He was the failure, and I was not. Failing would be staying in this miserable relationship where trust no longer lived. I thought that people were going to judge me. They were going to see me as a failure. However, I realized that anybody that cared about me was going to see I was in pain and that I deserved better."

TAKING CONTROL

With a broken heart, Katrina eliminated Mark from her life. She reached her lowest low. She felt unloved, defeated, and unworthy. She released everything she had bottled up. She cried, ate ice cream, watched movies, and truly felt her sadness. She faced her fear of feeling like a failure and embraced it. Katrina realized she did not deserve to stay with a man who did not respect her nor truly love her. She was not going to settle just because she wanted to follow a stupid timeline.

Katrina moved on to the healing process. She began with self-discovery. She sat down and decided what she truly desired in a relationship, a partner, life, and most importantly, herself. She quickly realized the original relationship "must haves" was a list that looked good according to societal standards but not her own. She was over other people telling her what to look for and strive for. She set her own rules. To ease her sadness, she traveled with her best friends and surrounded herself with positivity, and of course Ben & Jerry's.

To release her anger, she turned to fitness. She put herself first for the first time. She recalled getting a dose of self-love as she allowed herself to truly be vulnerable. Katrina mentioned, "Though it may seem like social media is the enemy at times, it's really the pressure we put on ourselves and what milestones we think we need to be hitting that's at fault. There's no need to feel humiliated by a relationship ending. The people who care about each of us don't care about our relationship status."

Katrina learned not to view the failure of a relationship as a defeat, but more like an empowering adventure. Being cheated on actually worked in her favor. She became stronger emotionally, physically, and mentally. Most importantly, Katrina realized the most important person she had to love was herself. She was the priority. "You don't get weaker with breakups. The more bad breakups I have had, the stronger I've become," she states, "I've rebuilt before. I'll do it again and again until I'm happy. Until I find someone worthy of my time. I'm worthy of my love."

Although she identified being cheated on as her biggest failure in love, but it truly became her biggest win. It taught her to be a proud, strong, independent woman who knows what she wants and deserves. She mentioned no longer following what society demands and living life through her own set of rules. Living by that attitude led her to meet her current partner. She is currently living a happy life beside a man who loves and respects her.

Just like Katrina, I think many people reach their lowest lows after a breakup. Feeling defeated and pained is normal. It has actually been proven the same brain areas are involved in physical pain and romantic rejection.[67] However, do not allow one heartbreak to tear you down. Life is too short to allow one failed relationship to rule your world. If your partner does not treat you with love and respect, then kick them to the curb. If a relationship suddenly ends, you will get through it. It is not the end of the world.

Everyone experiences a heartbreak at least once in a lifetime. No one is excluded in this. Katrina's mentality toward the approach of a heartbreak reminded me of Jennifer Lopez. JLo, a music icon, is widely known for her relationship history. She looks like a goddess, but even she has gone through a handful of heartbreaks. She has described, "If you look at it, yes the relationship ended, but look at how far you have come since your first heartbreak. If you are currently experiencing a heartbreak, I want to let you know you are strong, beautiful, and smart. This heartbreak is not going to be the end. You are just getting started as you will get back up and get back out there."[68]

---

67 Ethan Kross, Marc G. Berman, Walter Mischel, Edward E. Smith, Tor D. Wager, "Social Rejection Shares Somatosensory Representations With Physical Pain," *Proceedings of the National Academy of Sciences* 108, no.15 (April 2011): 6270-6275.

68 Nora Crotty, "Jennifer Lopez Talks About Being Cheated On," *ELLE*, last modified March 01, 2015.

JLo is right. Do not allow a heartbreak to hold you back. If you currently have a partner, think of the previous heartbreaks you had to go through to meet your current significant other. Every heartbreak leads you closer to the right person. After a breakup, pretend like it is December 31st and get ready for that New Year. Assess the relationship, examine the pros and cons, and decide what you would like to work on. Allow the situation to make you a better version of yourself. Once you find out what you want and what you are looking for, celebrate a new beginning! Grab yourself a mimosa to cheer on the new adventure.

As Katrina mentioned, picking yourself back up is the most enjoyable part. She advised, "You're going to wake up the next day and realize breakups aren't deadly; they're not permanent. It's not like you die if you break up with someone. You have this whole other life to live."

Party Favors:

- KNOW AND BELIEVE YOU ARE ENOUGH. A FAILED RELATIONSHIP DOES NOT DEFINE YOU.
- IF YOUR RELATIONSHIP ENDED, SEE IT AS AN OPPORTUNITY FOR A NEW ADVENTURE.
- BE KIND WITH YOURSELF. LOVE YOURSELF.
- DO NOT SETTLE. LIFE IS TOO SHORT TO SETTLE FOR A MEDIOCRE PARTNER.

CHAPTER 11:

TAKE RISKS

———

"Getting fired was the best thing that happened to me. Ten years later, here I am a VP at a major entertainment company and the co-host of the top morning show in Las Vegas."
—JOANNA DINATALE BAUMANN

Growing up we were told to work hard, stay in school, obtain a good job, and be successful. I remember hearing this multiple times from adults and thinking *getting to success sounds pretty easy.* To reach the mountain peak, I just had to follow those three steps. Well, I quickly found out that was a lie. One very important tidbit many people are not told about success is that failure comes alongside with it. I am thirty years old and I have experienced so much failure in my career I do not have enough fingers to count them all. I look back now and smile at every single one of them. Why? Well, because of them I proudly display manager, director, and vice president titles on my resume. Failure was not meant to destroy me; it was meant to make me stronger.

You get to the peak of the mountain by standing on the pile of your failures. I believe in this. For us to reach the top, we have to fail over and over again. As a manager, I always tell my team I want them to fail. Now, this does not mean do not reach your quota or blow a presentation. Quite the opposite. I want them to try new things, get out of their comfort zones, and strive for more. The earlier you fail, the more you learn. According to a study done by Northwestern University's Kellogg School of Management, "Failing early in your career could result in career success in the long run, stronger even than that of people who never had a setback."[69] The study analyzed scientists early in their careers who applied for research grants both those who obtained the grant and those who did not. The study tracked the amount of research papers produced by both groups. Dashun Wang, the study author, found those who failed to obtain the grant were 6.1 percent more likely to publish a "hit" paper than the successful ones.[70] The scientists who failed to obtain the grant had gone on to more successful careers in comparison to those who had won the grant.

Someone who is no stranger to this theory is Joanna DiNatale Baumann, a lady that has a combination of intelligence, skill, compassion, and commitment to community. If you thought the Las Vegas strip lights were bright and glamorous, you clearly have never met Joanna, iHeartMedia's vice president of marketing and partnerships in the Las Vegas market. If overseeing multiple departments for four radio stations was

69 Yang Wang, Benjamin F. Jones, Dashun Wang, "Early-Career Setback and Future Career Impact," Nature Communications 10, no.4331 (October 2019).

70 Ibid.

not enough, she also co-hosts on air in the mornings on Sunny 106.5. Although Joanna now sits in a beautiful, luxury office which oversees downtown Las Vegas, she didn't always have the best seat in the house.

FAIL EARLY

Her career took a turn when she got let go from the job she thought was going to take her to the next level. In connection to my personal experience of failures throughout my career, I was interested to learn how Joanna went advanced so fast and embraced the misfortune of losing a job. Joanna associates her ability to rise from failure with her secret weapon of turning every risk and rejection into an opportunity. I had the honor to personally sit with and interview Joanna as she preached her take on failure. "Do not linger in the sadness of failure. Turn it into an opportunity for whatever direction you want to go in," she advised.

Growing up in Chicago and loving heels, makeup. and the color pink, her career began in Claire's headquarter corporate offices. If you have never heard of Claire's before, it is teen's wonderland in a store. The store is full of an abundance of glittery objects and it takes a moment for your eyes to adjust to the shine. This store is covered in pink and colorful, bright, glittery accessories. I am talking tiaras, purses, scrunchies, earrings, and much more. I am not exaggerating when I say a blank wall does not exist in that store. It looks a bit chaotic, but the sparkle draws in young crowds. It most definitely drew in Joanna when she was given the opportunity to be part of their marketing team. She mentioned, "Working at Claire's headquarters was a dream first job. It was a great environment. It was fun. I love to be a girly-girl, so it was a home run."

She felt blessed to be given the opportunity to work at the head-quarters of the brand she grew up with. Joanna hit the ground running and immersed herself in the marketing world. She loved her team, was learning from professionals in the indus-try, and enjoyed every second of it. She had found her passion, until a year and a half later when she realized her growth in the company was stagnant. As a marketing coordinator, marketing manager would be the next promotion. However, like many corporate environments, you cannot move into a position if the spot is already filled. Joanna had to wait for a marketing manager to leave to continue up the ladder. She did not want to wait because, in her words, "As I began my career, I wanted as much experience as I possibly could get in the first five years. In order to do that, I told myself I'd stay at a job for about a year, year and a half, and then move on."

Although Joanna was very comfortable at Claire's, she was in search of a new challenge. She did not want to become a fashion buyer nor a fashion designer, so she decided to take a risk by leaving her safety net and stepping out of her comfort zone. She began to apply to other marketing jobs in the Chicago area to find a position she could gain more experience from. She wasn't married to a specific industry, but she was determined to stay in the marketing field. The search ended when she landed in the world of carpet and blinds with Empire Today. She states, "I left a very cushy job for a place totally unknown to me. I was going to make more money, and I was going to get out of my comfort zone to experience something new."

If you do not recall Empire Today's infamous television commercials, "Call 1-800-5-8-8-2-300 ... Empire Today,"[71] I will provide a quick summary of the company. First of all, glitter is not involved. Empire Today is a home improvement and furnishing company specializing in carpet, flooring, and window treatments. Stepping into Empire Today was completely out of Joanna's comfort zone. She went from princess wonderland to wooden floors and blinds. Although Joanna did not know one thing about home furnishings, the exciting challenge included more money and more experience to add to her resume. She was being challenged and learning something new every day. Until she hit her third month on the job and was asked to join a mandatory meeting with 30 percent of the company. The meeting's intention was to allow HR to announce everybody in the room was getting let go that day. The company was doing mass layoffs due to the recession the country was facing at the time. Just like Joanna was the last one in, she was the first one out. "I was hurt. I couldn't believe three months ago I had a job that I was happy and comfortable with, and now I was unemployed."

Joanna was devastated with the news. She took a risk with this new opportunity and failed. She remembered feeling regret for leaving Claire's and felt, "This was another kind of failure level for me. I was angry, sad, and needed to get a job again."

This all took place in 2008 when the country's economy faced a large drop, and big companies were cutting major

---

71   *Empire Today,* "Empire Carpet | Empire Today Commercial End Tag,"
     May 3, 2011, video, 0:07.

portions of their business to stay afloat. Due to hiring being very scarce at that time, she began to collect unemployment. She remembered being lost: "I didn't know where to go. I was applying to anything and everything I absolutely could, and at that point I really did feel hopeless. That was probably the darkest point in my life. I went through a few weeks of feeling bad for myself, but then I decided to change my attitude. I decided to take this failure and see it as a new opportunity—maybe somewhere new—and do something different."

Little did Joanna know her darkest moment would lead her to the best moments of her life in Las Vegas.

REJECTION TO OPPORTUNITY

Being sick of the cold Chicago winters, Joanna decided she was going to move to sunny Las Vegas. She did not have any connections in Las Vegas, nor did she know anyone, but the unknown factor excited her. She thought *new city, new opportunities.* She began to apply to every marketing coordinator position available. She did not hear back from anyone until three months later when she received a call from MetroPCS requesting an interview. According to Joanna, MetroPCS at the time was a new telecommunications company launching in Las Vegas. She didn't know anything about telecommunications, but she loved the city of Las Vegas and knew it would be a step toward a senior marketing coordinator position.

Upon completing the interview rounds, Joanna was offered the job and made her move to Las Vegas. She explained, "I took the chance and moved on my own. I never wanted to feel what I felt the day I got let go at Empire Today, so I promised I was going to meet everyone and anyone. I was going to shake so many hands in order to make something of myself in Las Vegas."

Although her friends and family warned her about the consequences and the risk, she ignored them. Joanna saw it as a new opportunity and put all her energy to make the best of it. Upon arriving, she did exactly what she had promised. She put herself out there and gave away her business cards like they were going out of style. Luckily, one recipient was a staff member of Clear Channel Broadcasting, the former name of what is now iHeartMedia.

After two years learning all about telecommunications with MetroPCS, Joanna found herself at an amazing company with great perks, but her growth was stagnant. Her marketing director was not going anywhere and the company did not have the funds to create a new position for her. Again, she was on the job sites in search of a new position. Due to Joanna wanting to advance in her career, she applied for every marketing manager position in Las Vegas. Before she knew it, she was starting as a marketing manager for the Riviera Hotel. "I knew it was taking a risk because it was an older hotel, but I was in the hospitality capital of the world. I thought, I could come in and share my fresh ideas. I thought it was going to be great!" Joanna explained.

The greatness did not quite get there. Eight months into the job, Joanna realized she had made a big mistake leaving MetroPCS. The job at the Riviera Hotel was not what she had hoped for, and she wanted out. Yet again, she felt like a failure. She moved to Las Vegas to work with an amazing company, but let it go and found herself in the same situation she had been in after being fired from Empire Today. She was back to square one and was desperate to find a new job. She reached out to all of those hands she had shaken and let them know her situation. Joanna was not shy to let her contacts understand she had made a mistake and needed help getting out. Luckily for her, that one contact from iHeartMedia responded to her message and informed her they were hiring for a director of marketing. She applied for the position and received an offer.

Upon getting hired with iHeartMedia, Joanna put all her energy into shaking every hand possible in the industry. She learned from her colleagues and went all in. She had finally found a position that challenged her and offered opportunities to continue to excel in her career. Upon wrapping up her third year, she was presented with the opportunity to become VP of the marketing department. Not only that, but she was also invited to become a co-host of the morning show on their station. She went from director to vice president and currently sits as the co-host of the top morning show in Las Vegas.

Joanna described, "Now I'm in a position in a city that I absolutely love, and it was because I had to lose the job at Empire Today. If I had stayed at Claire's, who knows where I'd be today. Timing in life, as cliché as it can sound, really always equates in the end to be the right thing, even if it's a dark point in your life."

Changing her attitude toward failure is what allowed Joanna to believe there were better opportunities, and she had to go out and chase them. She explained, "I look at failure and risks more as an opportunity and what can I take from this opportunity to really make myself what I inevitably want to be and know I can be."

As I interviewed Joanna and learned about her approach toward failure, it was reminiscent of Anna Wintour, another powerhouse of a lady who is no stranger to the bright lights of the media. The iconic editor-in-chief may have been highlighted in *Forbes'* "100 Most Powerful Women," but she was not always the *Vogue* boss she is now. Upon moving to the United States and being a junior fashion editor at *Harper's Bazaar*, Anna was fired nine months after starting the job. She began as fashion editor at the now defunct publication *Viva*, which folded a couple of years later. These setbacks did not stop Anna, as she went on to become the creative director and then editor-in-chief at *Vogue*.

Anna Wintour has stated, "Everyone should get sacked at least once. It forces you to look at yourself. It is important to have setbacks because that is the reality of life. Perfection doesn't exist."[72]

Both Joanna and Anna have the tenacity of viewing failure as new opportunities and not being afraid of taking risks. Getting fired turned out to be a blessing for these two. Remember, getting fired will not kill you. Getting fired is just a detour to a better destination.

---

72 Cara Alwill Leyba, "The Most Inspiring Career Quotes from Anna Wintour," Cara Alwill Leyba, accessed May 01, 2020.

Party Favors:

- FAILURE IN YOUR CAREER EQUALS TO NEW OPPORTUNITIES. DO NOT LET ONE SETBACK STOP YOU FROM REACHING SUCCESS. EVERYONE FAILS—WELCOME TO THE CLUB.
- TAKE RISKS AND GET OUT OF YOUR COMFORT ZONE. THE OPPORTUNITIES ARE ENDLESS. IT ALL COMES DOWN TO YOUR MOTIVATION TO CHASE THEM.
- FAILURE WILL NOT KILL YOU. FAILURE WILL KILL YOUR DREAMS ONLY IF YOU ALLOW IT.

CHAPTER 12:

PITY PARTY PEP TALK

———

"Promise me you'll always remember: You're braver than you believe, stronger than you seem, and smarter than you think."[73]

—A.A. MILNE, WINNIE THE POOH

I truly believe failure makes you stronger. Failure is part of the process. Some situations will be easier than others to overcome. Due to this, you may run into a situation requiring a little push or some hand holding to help you see the light at the end of the tunnel. This is where pep talks come in. Pep talks are my jam. Whenever I am feeling off and in need of a pick-me-up, I call my set of best friends. I could be having the worst day ever, but they each know exactly what to say to get me back on track. In honor of that, I would like to be your best friend and leave you with a pep talk to help you upon experiencing those unexpected life bumps.

———

73   Peter Economy, "17 Disney Quotes That Will Inspire You To Remarkable Success," *Inc.*, last modified March 22, 2017.

This is a pep talk from one Pity Partier to another. I like to begin all pep talks with some truth, so here it goes: I hope you fail. I hope life detours take you to unknown roads. I hope you fall down. Throughout this book, you have learned failures are the foundations to bigger successes. The sweetest victory is the most difficult one. It's the one that caused a couple of bruises and required you to reach deep inside and fight with everything you've got. This being said, I wish failure upon as much as I wish for you to gain the greatest success. I hope you chase and celebrate failure from now on and grow from it. Do not stay in your comfort zone to avoid setbacks. If you truly want to reach your end goal, you need to fight. Get comfortable with being uncomfortable. You have stood back up in the past, and you will continue to do so. You are strong and can overcome anything.

FAILURE HAS KEPT SOME GOOD COMPANY

You are not alone. Everyone has ridden the failure train and has experienced setbacks. After experiencing a negative condition in life, knowing that someone else has been there and surpassed the situation allows you to feel more at ease. I want to remind you that you are not the first person nor the last to fail. Let's go down memory lane, shall we? Did you know Oprah was fired from her first job in television?[74] Or that JK Rowling's *Harry Potter* manuscript was rejected by twelve major publishers?[75] Or that Michael Jordan did not make his high school's varsity

---

74 "Six Famous People who Failed before Succeeding," Propertyupdate.au, accessed May 16, 2020.

75 Ibid.

basketball team?[76] Each of these celebrities did not reach success on the first try. They all failed big time. News flash—we have all failed and will continue to do so. I recognize some setbacks will be greater than others, and some will also sting more. However, please know you are not alone. Don't despair because you are in good company.

LIFE DOES NOT OWE YOU ANYTHING

Life is not easy, and it is not intended to be. Do not fall into the entitlement trap and think life owes you. Honey, it does not. One thing that gets my blood boiling is people who whine and play the victim, yet do not take action. If this is you, please stop. I am not suggesting you bottle your feelings or avoid standing up for yourself. When life is unfair, it is good to voice your feelings. I am referring to the people who complain for weeks and months and do not move on. For those eternal complainers, you are throwing away energy that should be focused on something else. Wrap it up, and plan and execute.

You are alive and have a beating heart. Stop throwing away valuable time. The ticket to life is not guaranteed. We do not know how much time we have left on Earth, so stop wasting valuable time. Stand back up and keep going. As a true Pity Partier, allow yourself to feel those feelings. Go ahead and have good crying session. But afterward, get moving forward. Chop, chop!

---

76   "MICHAEL JORDAN DIDN'T MAKE VARSITY—AT FIRST," *Newsweek* Special Edition, *Newsweek*, last modified October 17, 2015.

BELIEVE IN YOURSELF

To be a successful Pity Partier and gain the benefits of failure, you must believe in yourself. You can do anything. Say it with me, "I can do anything." If nobody has told you lately, I am here to say I believe in you. You are smart, strong, and have the ability within yourself to surpass any failure life throws your way. Stop double-guessing yourself and self-sabotaging. Do not even allow yourself to go down that path. You have survived at least a dozen failures by now. Remember those times you thought there was no way to overcome the failures you were facing? Well, look at you now. You're still here. You figured it out. Take a glance back and see how much you have overcome. You've got this. Allow yourself to unlock your greatest potential. Believing in yourself is 100 percent up to you. I can cheer you along all day, but you have to believe in your own greatness. Only you have the power to achieve this.

CELEBRATE YOUR SUCCESSES

Give yourself credit for all your successes and truly celebrate them. Throughout the book I tell you to celebrate your failures. There is a reason Pity Party Number Two instructs you to do something that makes you happy. Give yourself credit for being a badass warrior. You can step out in the world and make things happen. Acknowledge your capability and triumphs. Talk about your achievements and do not be shy about it. If you want to show it off to the world on social media, more power to you. If you prefer to do it in silence, that is fine as well. Do whatever your heart desires. Take some time to pause and celebrate the amazing things you have achieved. Celebrating your wins not only feels amazing, but also reinforces the positive attitude and behavior you want to embrace when you face a new challenge.

BE A SUCCESSFUL FAILURE

Failure is not the end, instead, it is a detour to a new beginning. Upon experiencing failure, it may feel and seem like the world is coming to an end. If you ever find yourself feeling down, let me remind you of your strength. You are enough. Think of the countless others who have also failed. A great example is Walt Disney. When Walt Disney was fired from his job at the *Kansas City Star* in 1919, he was told by the editor of the paper that he "lacked imagination and had no good ideas." [77] That wasn't his last failure. Walt Disney later went on to purchase an animation studio named Laugh-O-Gram Studio, which he later drove into bankruptcy. Failure most certainly wasn't the end for Walt Disney, as we all know today. Many of the businesses and people we admire reach success because they did not allow failures stop them. No, they approached failures as a new beginning. I hope you do so as well. Remember, see failure as a new and exciting adventure. You've got this!

---

77 Eudie Pak, "Walt Disney's Rocky Road to Success," Biography, last modified June 27, 2019.

GOODBYE NEGATIVITY

"Other people's opinion is none of your business."[78]

—RACHEL HOLLIS

Forget about what others think of you and your failures. I understand failing may come with a sense of embarrassment or the typical "what are people going to say or think" thought that goes through your mind. But who cares? Other people will have opinions, that is the name of the game, but do not accept their negativity. Stay in your lane and anchor yourself on the end goal. You failed—great! Now focus on how you are going to get back up and try again. Tune out the derailing negativity. Other people can judge, but at the end of the day it is your life. You are the only one who decides if you are going to finish the race. Do not allow others to dictate your ending. Brush off the comments and continue forward.

---

78 *EdMylett*, "Watch this if you Struggle with Self-Doubt | Rachel Hollis," September 26, 2017, video, 58:40.

YOU'VE GOT THIS! PUT ON YOUR PARTY HAT

Upon experiencing failures or setbacks, throw yourself a Pity Party. Celebrate each of your failures and embrace the moment. If you look back and list out the top three failures you have experienced in your life, I guarantee they all led to where you are today. Take me for example. If I wouldn't quit, lost my job, and bombed certain work projects, I would not have gained all these opportunities in life. By making failure my friend, I have gained resilience and confidence. It helped me become the person I am today. That being said, do not hold yourself back from your greatest potential. Every failure is guiding you toward the road to success. You only have to believe it and believe in yourself.

Put on that party hat and throw yourself a Pity Party!

CONCLUSION:

THE AFTER PARTY

———

Life guarantees failure. You can try to avoid it, but avoiding failure would be to harmful to your growth. We all experience failure throughout our lives. Some will encounter it more than others, but the destination is the same. It is the road to success. Failure tends to be seen as a negative experience that destroys dreams and people's drive. No one wants to be labeled as a loser, as it certainly isn't an ego boost. I however, see failure as something to celebrate because failure is the foundation to bigger wins.

Failure has led me to my biggest victories. I am where I stand today due to the many setbacks I have experienced in my career and life. I have reached rock bottom and know what it feels like. I have also cried and been scared to try again. However, I have taught myself to be really good at standing back up and keep on going. Overcoming failure unleashes your greatest possibilities. It's sad to learn people allow fear of failure to stop them from reaching for their dreams. Your greatest wins live outside your comfort zone. Everyone has the potential to overcome every curveball. Some will be tougher than others, but it is possible. Failure needs to be approached effectively. Every time I meet someone who avoids failure or is too afraid to stand back up, I just want to hold their hand and teach them to embrace the situation. One door closing means two more open.

Failure should not be avoided. It should be chased and celebrated. Throughout this book I have walked you through my personal method of overcoming failure by using Pity Parties and becoming a true Pity Partier. I firmly believe you can overcome every failure thrown your way.

___

You are three Pity Parties away from your launch to the next step:

- **Pity Party One**: Feel your feelings.
- **Pity Party Two**: Do something that makes you happy.
- **Pity Party Three**: Learn the lesson and create a game plan to move forward.
- Wrap it up, stand back up, and keep going.

___

Pity Partiers embody various principles that allow them to stay grounded and motivated after experiencing challenging situations. As Sheila Bella taught us, failures are not to be personified and are only mistakes. Although Sheila faced many adversities, she never allowed failure to define her. She became comfortable with the process by burning the boat and not giving up when the sea turned choppy.

Pity Partiers are resilient; they do not get stuck in failure. Resilient Pity Partiers stand back up and keep moving forward. They believe in themselves and do not give up no matter how hard it gets. They view every failure as a new opportunity or, as my family says, *otra opportunidad*! Getting thrown off course means you have another opportunity to try again. Every failure can be seen as a step in a set of stairs. The more you fail and try again, the closer you get to the top.

As setbacks are experienced, you have to let go of the things you cannot control. I repeat, if you cannot control then let it go. We tend to want to push for things to happen our way and try to run the show. Life does not work that way. Do not focus on items outside of your control. Learn from the situation and move on. Concentrate on the good by practicing gratitude. We tend to get so caught up in the failure loop that we rarely pause and are thankful for the good that surrounds us. I encourage everyone to take a few minutes each day and look for three small things you are grateful for. Although it may feel like you are in the middle of the storm, I guarantee you can find a ray of beauty in the darkness.

Pity Partiers also allow rejection to sting a little bit. Embrace rejection and convert it into confidence. Create an assessment of the event or situation and learn from it. By doing this, it will allow you to react to rejection in a much more compassionate manner. Remember, self-negative talks are not allowed here. You are a resilient warrior, so act like one!

We also picked up additional principals with Katrina's experience of failure in love. She reminded us we are enough, and a failed relationship does not define who we are. Love yourself, be gentle, and see heartbreaks as a new adventure. Life is too short to settle. As Joanna taught us, take risks and get out of your comfort zone to find new opportunities. As Joanna failed during her career, we learned getting fired actually led to her successful career and executive position. Remember, failure will only kill your dreams if you allow it to.

You are in control of your life. This being said, I hope with the help of the Pity Party Method and the principals gained you will go out and chase failure. Celebrate every failure as a lesson to be learned. Do not give up. You are strong, smart, and can rise from any setback. I believe in you and wish you all the best.

While writing the book, I lived and experienced failure. I practiced every Pity Party Principle as I strived to complete every chapter and meet deadlines. I was reminded that failures are not fun. They are hard and even incite tears. However, taking the time to learn about every setback helped me get up and keep fighting. I consistently threw Pity Parties throughout my writing journey because writing and publishing a book is no joke. It was hard and frustrating, but I celebrated every setback, and look how far I have come. You now hold my finished product. I did it! Every tear, every missed happy hour, every deadline, and every long night was worth it.

This being said, my hope is you will apply the Pity Party Method next time you experience a failure. It allows you to alter your frame of mind as failure is introduced. I hope you better understand the importance of failing and failing often. The book was written with the intention to help those who want to surpass failure or those who want a better relationship with it. If you are feeling stuck, I hope I provided an easy framework with the three-step Pity Party Method. If you are ever in doubt of your potential, just remember: you are strong, smart, and are capable of anything. Show up for your life and keep going. You've got this!

APPENDIX

INTRODUCTION

- Ibañez Zadra Rose. "WHAT HAPPENS WHEN YOU FAIL?" Institute For Educational Advancement. Last modified April 10, 2018. https://educationaladvancement.org/blog-rewire-your-brain-for-success-when-you-fail/.

- Jacobson, Sheri. "Is this the Real Reason You Feel Like A Failure." *Harley Therapy Counselling Blog.* Last modified September 26, 2017. https://www.harleytherapy.co.uk/counselling/feel-like-a-failure.htm.

- National Institute of Mental Health. "Major Depression," Last Modified February 2019. https://www.nimh.nih.gov/health/statistics/major-depression.shtml.

- Premera Blue Cross. "Depression Diagnosis Rates are Increasing Across Washington, Study Finds." Last modified May 10, 2018. https://www.premera.com/visitor/press-releases/2018-05-10.

- Premier Health. "Beware High Levels of Cortisol, the Stress Hormone." Last modified February 05, 2017. https://www.premierhealth.com/your-health/articles/women-wisdom-wellness-/beware-high-levels-of-cortisol-the-stress-hormone.

CHAPTER 1

- Cameron Paula. "13 UPLIFTING QUOTES FOR A SHINY HAPPY NEW YEAR." Wall Art Prints (website). Last modified January 01, 2017. https://www.wallartprints.com.au/blog/uplifting-quotes/.

- *The Ed Sullivan Show.* "LESLEY GORE "It's My Party" on The Ed Sullivan Show." February 19, 2015. Video. 1:12. https://www.youtube.com/watch?v=lVwZhNx-_uQ.

CHAPTER 2

- *ABK Just Another Weblog.* "Fears Episode 13: Atychiphobia." *Penn State.* Last modified February 26, 2015. https://sites.psu.edu/akb13/tag/atychiphobia/.

- "About Resilience," Devereux Center For Resilient Children, Accessed May 27, 2020. https://centerforresilientchildren.org/home/about-resilience/.

- American Psychiatric Association. "What Is Depression." Depression. Accessed November 12, 2019. https://www.psychiatry.org/patients-families/depression/what-is-depression.

- Bruno, Karen, "Stress and Depression." WebMd, Accessed November 12, 2019. https://www.webmd.com/depression/features/stress-depression#1.

- Christopher Rosa and Leach Samantha. "12 Famous Women on Facing—and Overcoming—Failure." Glamour. Last modified January 29, 2019. https://www.glamour.com/story/famous-women-failure-quotes.

- Emel Bobbi, "Learning from Resilient Kids."Psych Central. Last modified October 08, 2018. https://psychcentral.com/lib/learning-from-resilient-kids/.

- Emerald Works. "Overcoming Fear of Failure Facing Your Fear of Moving Forward." Mind Tools. Accessed November 12, 2019. https://www.mindtools.com/pages/article/fear-of-failure.htm.

- Healthline. "Front Lobe," Accessed May 31, 2020. https://www.healthline.com/human-body-maps/frontal-lobe#1

- Hill Tamara. "Atychiphobia: 3 Signs You Fear Failure." Caregivers, Family & Friends. PsychCentral. Last modified December 04, 2018. https://blogs.psychcentral.com/caregivers/2018/12/atychiphobia-3-signs-you-fear-failure/.

- Ibañez Zadra Rose. "WHAT HAPPENS WHEN YOU FAIL?" Institute For Educational Advancement. Last modified April 10, 2018. https://educationaladvancement.org/blog-rewire-your-brain-for-success-when-you-fail/.

- Mauz Scott, "This Remarkable 32-Year Study of Kauai Islanders Reveals 7 Keys to Living a Resilient Life." *Inc.* Last modified June 13, 2018. https://www.inc.com/scott-mautz/this-remarkable-32-year-study-of-kauai-islanders-reveals-7-keys-to-living-a-resilient-life.html.

- Merriam-Webster Dictionary. s.v. "resilience (n.)." Accessed April 16, 2020. https://www.merriam-webster.com/dictionary/resilience.

- National Institute of Mental Health. "Major Depression." Last Modified February 2019, https://www.nimh.nih.gov/health/statistics/major-depression.shtml.

- *Rachel Hollis.* "The BEST Way To Start The New Year in 2020." December 26, 2019. Video. 3:46. https://www.youtube.com/watch?v=6NalzB6ZdH4.

- Scott Elizabeth, "All About Acute Stress What You Should Know About Acute Stress." VeryWellMind. Last modified April 08, 2020. https://www.verywellmind.com/all-about-acute-stress-3145064.

- Scott Elizabeth. "How Does Chronic Stress Negatively Affect Your Health?" VeryWellMind. Last Modified October 10, 2019. https://www.verywellmind.com/chronic-stress-3145104.

- Sroykham Watchara, and Yodchanan Wongsawat. "Effects of Brain Activity, Morning Salivary Cortisol, and Emotion Regulation on Cognitive Impairment in Elderly People." *Medicine* vol. 98,26 (2019): e16114. https://www.ncbi.nlm.nih.gov/pmc/articles/PMC6616250/#R10.

- Walter Ekaterina. "30 Powerful Quotes on Failure." *Forbes.* Last modified December 30, 2013. https://www.forbes.com/sites/ekaterinawalter/2013/12/30/30-powerful-quotes-on-failure/#7bea4e9d24bd.

- Winch Guy, "10 Signs That You Might Have Fear of Failure." *Psychology Today.* Last modified June 18, 2013. https://www.psychologytoday.com/us/blog/the-squeaky-wheel/201306/10-signs-you-might-have-fear-failure.

CHAPTER 3
- Sheila Bella. "SHEILA BELLA Founder & Lead Artist." Accessed April 17, 2020. https://www.sheilabellamakeup.com/sheila-bella.

CHAPTER 4
- Allan Patrick. "Jim Carrey on Why You Shouldn't Fear Failure." Failure. Lifehacker. Last modified. July 23, 2014. https://lifehacker.com/jim-carrey-on-why-you-shouldnt-fear-failure-1609703005.

- Hardy Benjamin. "23 Michael Jordan Quotes That Will Immediately Boost Your Confidence." *Inc.* Last modified April 05, 2016. https://www.inc.com/benjamin-p-hardy/23-michael-jordan-quotes-that-will-immediately-boost-your-confidence.html.

- Kierbow Harry. "7 Famous Quotes on Failure and the Stories That Inspired Them." GoSmallBiz. Last modified April 15, 2015. https://gosmallbiz.com/7-famous-quotes-on-failure-and-the-stories-that-inspired-them/.

CHAPTER 5

- Andersen Erika. "21 Quotes From Henry Ford On Business, Leadership And Life." *Forbes*. Last Modified May 31, 2013. https://www.forbes.com/sites/erikaandersen/2013/05/31/21-quotes-from-henry-ford-on-business-leadership-and-life/#f74ec5293c55.

- *ELLE Australia*. "Quotes On Failure (And Overcoming It) From Women Who've Succeeded Despite Their Hurdles." Culture. Last modified September 25, 2016. https://www.elle.com.au/culture/quotes-on-failure-and-overcoming-it-from-inspirational-women-8406.

CHAPTER 6

- Brian Tracy Quotes. BrainyQuote.com. BrainyMedia Inc. 2020. Accessed April 23, 2020. https://www.brainyquote.com/quotes/brian_tracy_125679.

- Wanderlust Worker. "Life Is 10% What Happens To You And 90% How You React." Accessed April 23, 2020. https://www.wanderlustworker.com/life-is-10-what-happens-to-you-and-90-how-you-react/.

CHAPTER 7

- "Acute Lymphoblastic Leukemia (ALL)." St. Jude Children's Research Hospital. Accessed April 25, 2020. https://www.stjude.org/disease/acute-lymphoblastic-leukemia-all.html.

- The Global Eagles. "Oprah's Gratitude Journal Oprah's Lifeclass Oprah Winfrey Network." October 26, 2013.

Video. 3:38. https://www.youtube.com/watch?time_
continue=8&v=saZWjIlwU8c&feature=emb_title.

- *TEDx Talks.* "Two words that can change your life | Tanmeet
  Sethi | TEDxRainier." February 16,2017. Video, 16:47.
  https://www.youtube.com/
  watch?list=RDCMUCsToYIqwnpJCM-mx7-
  gSA4Q&v=HHTmiHB6aXk&feature=emb_rel_end.

CHAPTER 8

- Adams R.L.. "21 Famous Failures Who Refused to Give Up."
  HUFFPOST. Last modified September 16, 2017.
  https://www.huffpost.com/entry/21-famous-failures-who-
  refused-to-give-up_b_57da2245e4b04fa361d991ba.

- Ercolano Patrick. "Don't Get Mad, Get Creative: Social
  Rejection Can Fuel Imagination, JHUCarey Researcher
  Finds." Johns Hopkins University. Last modified August 21,
  2012.
  https://releases.jhu.edu/2012/08/21/dont-get-mad-get-
  creative-social-rejection-can-fuel-imagination-jhucarey-
  researcher-finds/.

- Florio Angelica. "Need a Confidence Boost? Try Failing."
  Next Big Idea Club. Last modified December 08, 2015.
  https://nextbigideaclub.com/katty-kay-and-claire-shipman-
  failure-can-help-boost-confidence/2588/.

- Maraboli Steve. "You're Not Rejected – You're Redirected."
  Steve Maraboli. Accessed on May 25, 2020. https://
  stevemaraboli.net/youre-not-rejected-youre-redirected/.

- Turbull Brad. "Inspirational Quotes." The Mindset Journey. Last modified June 07, 2017. https://www.themindsetjourney. com/inspirational-quotes/become-so-confident-in-who-you-are-that-no-ones-behavior-opinion-or-rejection-can-affect-you-brad-turnbull/.

- Weir Kristen. "The Pain Of Social Rejection." *Monitor on Psychology* 43, no. 4(2012): 50. https://www.apa.org/monitor/2012/04/rejection.

CHAPTER 9

- Crow Sarah. "This Is Why You Need a "Happy Place"—and Where to Find It." Best Life. Last Modified October 26, 2013. https://bestlifeonline.com/find-your-happy-place/.

- The Harvard Gazette. "Winfrey's Commencement Address." Last Modified May 31, 2013. https://news.harvard.edu/gazette/story/2013/05/winfreys-commencement-address/.

- Layous Kristin, Chancellor Joseph, and Lyubomirsky Sonja. "Positive Activities as Protective Factors Against Mental Health Conditions." *Journal of Abnormal Psychology* 123. no. 1 (2014): 3-12. http://sonjalyubomirsky.com/files/2012/09/Layous-Chancellor-Lyubomirsky-2014.pdf.

- Nelson Noelle , Malkoc Selin A, and Shiv Baba. "Emotions Know Best: The Advantage of Emotional versus Cognitive Responses to Failure." *Behavioral Decision Making* 31. no. 1 (January 2018): 40—51. https://onlinelibrary.wiley.com/doi/abs/10.1002/bdm.2042.

- *Rachel Hollis.* "2020 Goal Setting | Rachel Hollis." January 14, 2020. Video. 47:46. https://www.youtube.com/watch?v=7JG34JHRcIg.

CHAPTER 10

- Cleveland Clinic. "Grieving After a Break-Up? 6 Strategies to Help You Heal." Metal Health. Last modified January 23, 2019. https://health.clevelandclinic.org/grieving-after-a-break-up-6-strategies-to-help-you-heal/.

- Crotty, Nora. "Jennifer Lopez Talks About Being Cheated On." *ELLE.* Last Modified March 01, 2015. https://www.elle.com/culture/news/a27051/jennifer-lopez-cheating-words-of-wisdom/.

- Kross, Ethan, Berman, Marc G., Mischel, Walter. Smith, Edward E, Wager, Tor D. "Social Rejection Shares Somatosensory Representations With Physical Pain." *Proceedings of the National Academy of Sciences* 108. no.15 (April 2011): 6270-6275. https://www.pnas.org/content/108/15/6270.abstract.

CHAPTER 11

- *Empire Today.* "Empire Carpet | Empire Today Commercial End Tag." May 3,2011. Video, 0:07. https://www.youtube.com/watch?v=uwJQQuxoTFo.

- Leyba Cara Alwill. "The Most Inspiring Career Quotes from Anna Wintour." Cara Alwill Leyba (blog). Accessed May 01, 2020. http://caraalwill.com/the-most-inspiring-career-quotes-from-anna-wintour/.

- Wang Yang, Jones Benjamin F., Wang Dashun. "Early-career setback and future career impact." Nature Communications 10. No.4331 (October 2019). https://www.nature.com/articles/s41467-019-12189-3#citeas.

CHAPTER 12

- Economy Peter. "17 Disney Quotes That Will Inspire You To Remarkable Success." *Inc.* Last modified March 22, 2017. https://www.inc.com/peter-economy/17-disney-quotes-that-will-inspire-you-to-remarkable-success.html.

- *EdMylett.* "Watch this if you Struggle with Self-Doubt | Rachel Hollis. September 26, 2017."Video, 58:40. https://www.youtube.com/watch?v=Yv54-P9Qyf8&t=1569s.

- *Newsweek.* "MICHAEL JORDAN DIDN'T MAKE VARSITY—AT FIRST." Newsweek Special Edition. Last modified October 17, 2015. https://www.newsweek.com/missing-cut-382954.

- Pak Eudie. "Walt Disney's Rocky Road to Success." Biography. Last Modified June 27, 2019. https://www.biography.com/news/walt-disney-failures.

- Propertyupdate.au."Six famous people who failed before succeeding." Accessed May 16, 2020. https://propertyupdate.com.au/six-famous-people-who-failed-before-succeeding/.

ACKNOWLEDGMENTS

This is my favorite part of the book! This is where I get to thank everyone who made this crazy book idea a reality. When setting out on this journey I've never embarked on before, I didn't know how much work and time it would take to reach the final destination. I've discovered during my journey writing *Pity Partiers* that publishing a book takes a ginormous village. I am forever grateful for the support, as this wouldn't have been possible without everyone who helped this book idea become a reality.

First and foremost, I'd like to thank my family for the endless love, support, lessons, and tools you have given me throughout my life. Mom and Dad, thank you for showing me how to be a good person with a big heart and how to treat others with kindness. Brother Bear, thank you for always believing in me and encouraging me to chase my dreams. Mom, thank you for teaching me that girls can do anything! The woman I am today is because of your love, dedication, care, guidance, and wisdom.

I've spent the last six months researching, writing, or editing this book. It has been half a year of outlines, verbal processes, stress, and sleepless nights to meet deadlines. Therefore, I want to thank my friends who have put up with all of my venting, crying sessions, and ditching out of happy hour early because I had to go write or edit. Thank you for the support, encouraging words, and love I received from you all.

Thank you to all of my interviewees. Thank you for taking time out of your busy schedules to share your stories. You all are badass queens!

A *major* thank you to New Degree Press, especially Eric Koester and all the amazing editors.

Lastly, I'd like to recognize everyone else who is not mentioned for all their contributions to help me make this book a reality:

Carla Linares
Andy and Bholi Narang
Dylan Kenyon
Namrata Dhingreja
Mariko Anderson
Julia McCarthy
Mike Harms
Stilianos Panos
Kim Charbeneau
Aaron Ramos
Lauren Steverson
Jazzmin Martinez
Ashley Sain
Shane Johnson
Melissa Hutapea
Paulina Linares
*Demetri Gus

Sarah Perez
*Knock Rentals
Kristin Poleski
Kristen Herlosky
Elizabeth Baldivias
Maile Eubank
Toby Yuen
Candice Rochelle
Andrew Soliven
Anna Angerman
Karen Avila
Cory Blyth
Li Zhang
Loren Jobe
Kiara Akpore
Michelle Reyes
Camdra Garcia
Erica Pelayo
Mary Sholly
Kaylee Meyer
~Joanna Baumann
Jacopo Gardini
Rishikesh Yardi
Tamara Martinezjunco
Julia Fox
Maria Hanes
Andrea Benites
Mikaela Kasalek
Michal Davis
Bianca Johnson
George Plumis
Sandra Ramirez

Rebecca Robles
Ann Frisbie
Dustin Hawley
Roland Santos
Jim Blake
Alycia Anderson
Darlene Pelayo
Amy St. Louis
Michele Bonenfant
Megan Trejo
Mercedes Sanchez
Hayley Miller
Ashley Ledford
Hanna Hilts
Jesus Campuzano
Karuna Narang
Tim O'Connor
Katrina Concepcion
Janina Loyola
Michael Moon
Nikolina Kosanovic
Jorge Carrasco
Eric Koester
Tara Ritchey
Kaylie Garcia
Mandy Ward
Anatoli Pavlov
Maria Alonso

CPSIA information can be obtained
at www.ICGtesting.com
Printed in the USA
LVHW080312040920
665083LV00023B/3183